The Cross in the Sawdust Circle

a theology of clown ministry

by Dick Hardel

YOUTH & FAMILY INSTITUTE
of AUGSBURG COLLEGE

Minneapolis, Minnesota
www.youthfamilyinstitute.com

The Cross in the Sawdust Circle

Author: Dr. Dick Hardel
Editor: Carolyn Berge
Photos: Cindy Bailey, Carolyn Hardel, James Kashork, Randall Williams
Cover design: Jennifer Leonardson at Meirovitz & Company
Interior design: Carolyn Berge

The scriptural quotations in this book are taken from the New Revised Standard Version of the Bible (NRSV). Copyright © 1989 by the Division of Christian Education of the National Council of the Churches of Christ in the United States of America. All rights reserved.

ISBN 1-889407-44-5

Published by the Youth & Family Institute of Augsburg College, Minneapolis, Minnesota 55454-1351. All rights reserved. No part of this book may be reproduced by any means without written permission of the publisher.

Printed in the United States of America.

This book is dedicated to
the memory of Mark "Tony" Anthony

Clown Hall of Fame 1989
Friend and Teacher
Child of God

Contents

foreword

The Cross in the Sawdust Circle is a journey into the center of faith. One picture of God is a circle, sometimes the circumference and sometimes the center. The church clown practices the meaning of faith in the center and the circumference. The spotlight for clowning is on the cross. That is what is to be seen.

The author is focused on the Spirit of God, breathed into Adam and into us all. The clown's highest goal is to be filled with that Spirit, to let it decorate the body and to give the clown a new name. Clowns are full of the colors of life and they have a new name. This book will show that this is true with us all.

Three types of clowns live in the circle of God: the auguste clown, the whiteface clown, and the hobo clown. All clowns find home in these persons. So the Christ clowns are birthed in Christmas. There is an Epiphany clown filled with vision of the glory of God manifest in Christ Jesus. This clown journeys from Epiphany to Ash Wednesday. There is a Lenten clown who lives on the fringes of life in ashes and sackcloth, yet walks in hope from Ash Wednesday to the Easter Vigil. There is an Easter clown who journeys from the empty cross through the empty tomb into all of life. These clowns unfold the spirit of us all, who live in the seasons of life, the church year, and faith. Dick Hardel opens this faith journey for us all—clowns and would-be clowns.

The Cross in the Sawdust Circle opens an inquisitive spirit for people of faith. People of the Cross ask a clowning question,

"What does this mean?" The Christ clown asks, "What do you see? What is God saying to you? What do you want to do?" A Christ clown carries a message, delivers a gift, and we get to open the good news.

In clown ministry, Hardel has mastered the style of parable, metaphor. The clown routines raise questions of meaning: "Who am I to God? Who am I? Who are we to each other?" Hardel leads the readers to find the inquisitive spirit of Christ's language in each other.

Dick Hardel is a veteran clown. Thousands have experienced the meaning of this good book in many countries through the ministry of a clown. The book is true in any language or culture. Clown is a language for all ages. It is a language that does not need an answer.

The Cross in the Sawdust Circle is fabric, poetic, biblical, whole, and enables readers to experience weaving Word and world. The clown in the circle is arting the faith, creatively expressing the faith. It is a holy act under a very big tent with the cross as the center pole. Hardel helps take the reader into a great circus cathedral where people of all ages experience the greatest story ever lived. Clown connects the stories of life to the Word.

In this book God is revealed as gardener, parent, musician, theologian, and Spirit. Many of the findings of the Youth & Family Institute of Augsburg College that Hardel serves as executive director give power and reality to this reading. These pages are profound, down to earth, in the sawdust, under the cross, in the circle, with each other, and of the Spirit. The book is about the gospel of Jesus Christ in color, motion, laughter, and delight. Throughout these pages Dick pictures faith in silent images, theology.

The author believes God created us to art the grace of God. Hardel knows this spirit of arting faith by heart.

The Cross in the Sawdust Circle is a book for clowns, would-be clowns, clergy, teachers, families, youth leaders, religion professors, and preachers. Hardel will help you look again and again at meanings of the gospel in a circle we know as body of Christ.

This book may make you a clown. It will show you how God's breath, God's Spirit, lives inside us; we are Christ's clowns, clumps of earth with breath. We are the earth into which God breathes Spirit.

Read the book as though each page is happening to you. Read slowly and imagine what you read as real in your life. Identify with the insights. Find the difference and relation of church and circus clown. Find the mantle of the church clown who is a fool for Christ.

The Cross in the Sawdust Circle is a theological document that reads like a stained-glass window.

—*Herbert Brokering*

Introduction

The Youth & Family Institute of Augsburg College proudly presents *The Cross in the Sawdust Circle*! "What's with that? What possible connection could there be between a book on clown ministry and an institute dedicated to strengthening families and congregations in faith formation?"

It is a great question. I'm glad you asked. "Sawdust circle" is a term used for the circus. Sawdust was laid down on the ground within the performing ring or rings of the circus. It provided a soft cushion for the animals and even for some of the performers, and it absorbed the moisture and smells left by the animals. So phrases like "sawdust in your blood" or the "smell of sawdust in the air" are references to the circus being part of one's life, to the dedication of a person to bringing joy and laughter to children of all ages. The circus, sideshows, and carnivals are often understood as being very secular and earthy places. The cathedral might be thought of as being the total opposite of the big top of the circus.

The cross is the symbol for the heart of the message of the Christian church to the world. Through the death and resurrection of Jesus Christ, the Creator God has redeemed human beings and all the rest of a fallen creation. This Creator God brings us into a new relationship of love, joy, peace, hope, and faith. God calls us to live closely with one another. To put a cross in the sawdust circle is to say that people can find the sacred in the secular. What makes anything holy is the presence of God. Through the cross of Jesus we see the whole world differently. This cross is not just for the cathedrals but for every place of everyday living. When we limit holiness and God to specific places, we end up with a very narrow theology. Then our faith in and understanding of God is in a box, separated from the realities of our lives.

The Youth & Family Institute of Augsburg College is dedicated to the strengthening of families and congregations to pass on the faith in Jesus Christ to the next generations. We should not only think of God and talk about God when we are in church buildings. To pass on the faith it is important for congregations to work in partnership with the home in teaching and nurturing faith. The home is the domestic church, and our God is present in all of life—our workplaces, schools, neighborhoods, hospitals, and vacation places. The Institute provides training for church leaders and parents to gain critical skills in passing on the faith. The Youth & Family Institute of Augsburg College is dedicated to bringing joy and laughter through the gospel of Jesus Christ to all generations of people. The Institute encourages congregations to do intergenerational ministries outside the walls of the church buildings.

The ministries of Christian congregations outside their own walls should make a difference in the quality and longevity of the lives of the people in those communities. The gospel of Jesus Christ offers forgiveness and wholeness to fractured people. Laughter and joy are signs of healthy and whole relationships. Of all places where there needs to be laughter, playfulness, and joy, it is in the homes of the people of God. The Youth & Family Institute of Augsburg College teaches four keys for nurturing faith and whole family relationships:

1. Caring Conversation. Christian values and faith are passed on to the next generation through supportive conversation. Listening and responding to the daily concerns of our children make it easier to have meaningful conversations regarding the love of God and ways to express God's love to others.

2. Family Devotions. Adults need to learn the Christian message and the biblical story as their own story if they are to pass on their faith to their children and other adults. Our Christian faith shapes the whole of our lives and involves a lifetime of study, reflection, and prayer.

3. Family Rituals and Traditions. Families identify themselves and tell their family stories through daily routines, celebrations, and rituals. Whether it's an annual summer vacation, the hanging of Christmas ornaments, or an informal liturgy before bedtime, these activities speak volumes about what the family values, believes, and promotes, and how much a family values its faith.

4. Family Service. Children, youth, and adults are most likely to be influenced by those who "walk the talk." There are many opportunities for service: some in the congregation, some in the larger community. Whatever service is chosen, it is best done with family members or other intergenerational groups.

The Cross in the Sawdust Circle is a book on the theology of clown ministry. It suggests that a clown may be the best tool in ministry of the 21st century to bring busy people to a halt, to wonder, and to see the sacred in the midst of the secular of everyday life. This is more than having a clown entertain at a birthday party. This is about seeing God in all of life. The clown helps people see God in all of the milestones of family life. Some family milestones are joyous and others are very painful. By creating word pictures of the gospel, the clown brings the healing power of laughter and play to people who are out of breath.

Healthy families breathe well and laugh well. The Youth & Family Institute of Augsburg College brings in the clowns and proudly presents *The Cross in the Sawdust Circle*.

Preface

All my life I have loved the circus and the Christian church. I may have been baptized in the Christ event with both water and sawdust. I grew up in Milwaukee, Wisconsin, where Christian churches abound and Ringling Bros. and Barnum & Bailey® Circus once led a parade every Fourth of July. Our family loved to laugh and play. We attended worship every Sunday and midweek services during Advent and Lent. When a circus came to town, we attended it. In the circus I loved the clowns and the elephants. In the church I loved to sing and hear the great stories of faith from the Bible. I grew up thinking that there was a connection between the Christian church and the circus.

It took me 29 years to begin formally working with the connection of the cross and the sawdust circle, the Christian church and the circus. It began in 1973 when I was a Lutheran pastor of three small, rural congregations in South Dakota. I traveled with the youth from the three rural congregations to the All Lutheran Youth Gathering in Houston, Texas. At this gathering of 20,000 Lutheran youth we met clowns who had been brought in to interpret some of the large stage events and to direct the crowds to the right places. I was fascinated at how a clown could communicate to a group of even 100 people and keep them connected. From that moment on I tried to learn as much as I could about the circus and the role of the clown. Anytime I found people who were clowns in the circus I visited them, sat at their feet, and listened to them tell about the American circus and being a clown.

I was blessed by God's call for me to move to Florida and serve congregations there. The Cole Bros. and Clyde Beatty Combined Circus wintered in Deland, Florida. The Ringling Museum was in Sarasota. Ringling Bros. and Barnum & Bailey Circus wintered in Venice, Florida. The Clown College was also in Venice and for a few years Circus World was in Haines City, Florida. I had many opportunities to learn more about the art of clowning and the history of the American circus.

I started using clowning in my ministry in 1973, but I didn't know much about being a clown or using the art of clowning in ministry. I kept searching for those who could teach me more,

and I read every book on clowning and clown ministry I could find. In 1977 I started teaching clown ministry skills to high school youth in the congregation and created Christ Clown College. I still did not know much about the art of clown ministry. There I started my first clown troupe, The Life In Christ

Circus. No matter where God called me to serve as pastor I continued to teach others the theology and art of clown ministry.

The more I met circus clowns and other church clowns, the more I knew I didn't know much. I was always open to learn. Circus clowns taught me so much. I learned how to juggle from Ron Severini. He also taught me how to market anything. Wayne Sidley taught me how to stage clown gags and how to be a boss clown. Wayne Scott taught me how to make props and how to love a good friend. I learned mime skills and routines to practice facial expressions and body expressions from Billy Scadlock. I learned about the loyalty of close friends and how to love the audience from Leon McBryde. Jim Howle taught me about seeing the clown within another person and helping them develop that character. But I learned about the heart of a clown and how to love as a clown from Mark "Tony" Anthony. Steve "T. J. Tatters" Smith taught me how to respect the audience and to know the history of clowning and study the art of clowning. As you can see, I was blessed by God to learn from great clowns, many of them in the Clown Hall of Fame. From the clown ministry skills of the Rev. Floyd Shaffer I learned to make more connections between the cross and the sawdust circle.

As blessed as I was to have met and learned about clowning from such great people, I was even more blessed to have been raised by Christian parents. I learned about the love of Jesus Christ and the Bible stories of a faithful and gracious God from my mother. My mother taught me how to love people and live the gospel in relationship with other people. I learned to grow deeper in faith from my childhood pastor and friend, Dr. John F. Johnson. He has always been my model for being a good pastor and a faithful teacher of the Bible. My Greek professor, Dr. Walter Bartling, taught me about the humanity and divinity of Christ, how to be a good exegete, and to open myself to the Word of God. Dr. Norman Habel, professor of Old Testament theology, taught me about the prophetic role of ministry and how do be creative in demonstrating the message of the Word of God. From

Dean Dammann, Eldor Kaiser, and Leo Symmank I learned how to use my creative gifts in youth ministry. The list of gifted people—those who have helped me to learn how to connect the cross with the sawdust circle—goes on and on. I know I must grow deeper in my faith and ministry.

Herbert Brokering and Penne Sewall are my two amigos in clown ministry. My friend Herb is the most creative person I have

ever met. He is a visionary of the Christian church and a vulnerable lover of people. Although he has never put on makeup, he is the heart and soul of a clown. From Herb I learned how to live life inside-out. Penne is a marvelously gifted clown. Her graceful motions, creative thinking, and loving heart brings one into the presence of God. We continually plan and strategize how to give this clown ministry away to the Christian church in eastern Europe.

The writing of this book comes out of my discoveries that for me to be effective in ministry, I must keep growing deeper in my theology and my practice of my faith. I do believe the clown can be a wonderful symbol and tool for the church as it grows through the challenges of the 21st century. But to be effective, church clowns must grow deeper in the theology of clown ministry, knowledge of the history of the church and the circus, and gain skills of communicating the gospel of Jesus Christ. There are not many resources in clown ministry that focus on a theology of clown ministry. One can find a chapter or a few pages written on theology, but not an entire book.

So in 1988 I published my first book on the theology of clown ministry, *Welcome to the Sawdust Circle Part I*. Later that year I published my second book, *Welcome to the Sawdust Circle*

Part II: Learning the Art of Clown Ministry. My first book has been out of print for about six years. I noticed that there still are not many books written on the theology of clown ministry since I wrote my first book. I had intended to simply rewrite my first book. But as I began, it became a whole new book.

The Cross in the Sawdust Circle is written for church clowns to strengthen their theological understanding of clown ministry. It is written for non-clowns as well as clowns to learn more about the church and more about the circus. It is written for leaders of the church to learn about the active symbol of the clown as it moves in ministry through the 21st century. It is written as an invitation for more people to join in the foolishness of God and celebrate life.

chapter 1

Connecting the church & the circus

Once there was a man who sold balloons. A church bought 250 every Sunday. When it was 10:45, he would always enter and let them fly among the people. They would hit them and laugh. Every time they hit a balloon, they shouted alleluia. That was the only thing they did: Hit and shout alleluia. The air was full of color and balloons, and it was full of alleluia sounds. It is called balloon sounds in the bulletin. They are trying it out this year to see if it works.[1]

W hy would a church invite clowns to help lead a worship service? Why would anyone ever bring a cross into the sawdust circle of the circus? What could the circus learn from the church and what could the church learn from the circus? What possible connection could there be between a circus and a church? Circus and church, Big Bertha and Mt. Olivet, Big Top and cathedral—they seem so opposite each other.

The circus seems so secular. The music is loud and blaring; the colors and costumes are bright and gaudy. The circus is filled with fascinating fantasy as bright, shining spotlights point out the stars. In the area of the circus the people laugh, clap their hands, and are joyous. The circus is filled with "ooh"s and "aah"s as

---

1 Herbert Brokering, *I Opener* (St. Louis, Mo.: Concordia Publishing House, 1974), p. 44.

well as "ha! ha! ha!"s. The circus program is splashed with all the bright colors of the rainbow, and every performing act is introduced with exaggerated hype:

VENTURESOME VAULTING VIRTUOSITY

Europe's Far-Famed And Fabled Family Of Passionately Perspicacious Performers Eloquently Exhibit Estimable Elephantine Erudition And Abundant Acrobatic Astuteness; Superb, Scintillating Skills That Commandingly Captured The Coveted Silver Clown Award At The International Circus Festival Of Monte Carlo!

HUNGARY'S RENOWNED ROYALTY OF THE RING
THE REMARKABLE RICHTERS[2]

In contrast, many leaders of Christian churches seem to believe that laughter, joy, and applause are not reverent or proper in worship or in ministry. To them the worship of our holy God needs to be quiet, humble, and respectful of an awesome God. A holy God needs holy worship. *Holy* to them means serious. Some Christian people are so serious about what worship should be and what they believe God expects, that they turn the gospel into a series of laws. So worship to them is following a set of rules. This seriousness of life causes some people to divide all of life into two categories: sacred and secular. The secular is viewed as bad, wrong, and devoid of the presence of God. But they are certain that God is at home in the sacred, reverent rituals of the sacred. Sacred is viewed as good, right, and filled with the presence of God. Thus certain types of music, types of instruments, colors, symbols, even buildings are judged to be either sacred—thus, with God's approval—or secular, and thus with God's disapproval. The sacred is for the serious, heavy heart. The secular is for the light-hearted.

Far too often in serious worship the "ooh"s and "aah"s are replaced with "zzz"s. The order of service and the announce-

2 Act #11 from the 110th Edition Souvenir Program and Magazine of Ringling Bros. and Barnum & Bailey Combined Shows, Inc., 1980.

ments of a Christian worship service are usually printed in serious, black ink on white paper:

WORKCAMPERS' FUNDRAISER
Friday, Feb. 9, 2001: Spaghetti Dinner and Variety Show.
Dinner begins at 6:00 p.m. & Variety Show is at 7:00
p.m. Tickets will be sold on Sunday mornings through
Feb. 7. Contact Shannon Smith if you would like to be in
the variety show! All acts are welcome.[3]

It is easy to point out more differences and reasons why it may be very difficult for circus people to understand a cross standing in the sawdust circle of the center ring and for church people to see the ring of circus sawdust surrounding the cross in their cathedrals. In my first book on clown ministry, *Welcome to the Sawdust Circle Part I*, I shared more detail of my research on the differences.[4] But I think we gain more here by focusing on what the circus and the church have in common. Circus clowns might learn that there may be more room for clowns in the church than presently in the circus. And the church just might discover a way to live out every day in the joy of Easter. Cal Samra in *The Joyful Christ, The Healing Power of Humor* shares a quote of the Rev. Floyd Shaffer that expresses this point so well:

Shaffer's alter ego, Soccataco, has observed, "The Christian church has all the language of a party, but hasn't been able to pull it off."[5]

Traditionally, the Christian church chose Sunday for worship services as a reminder that every Sunday is a little Easter. Even the Sundays during the season of Lent are not counted in the

3 Taken from an actual congregation where I was the guest preacher. Only the name has been changed.
4 Dick Hardel, *Welcome to the Sawdust Circle Part I: A Theology of Clown Ministry* (Orlando, 1988), pp. 13-17.
5 Cal Samra, *The Joyful Christ: The Healing Power of Humor* (San Francisco, CA: Harper & Row Publishers,1985), p. 46.

forty days of Lent. Often the seriousness of our view of God and making certain that everyone and everything are in their right places for worship gets in the way of the central theology of the Christian church—grace. Grace is a theology of the cross of Jesus Christ standing in the middle of the sawdust circle of life. God has done it all in Jesus. All the people who believe in this gospel of Jesus Christ can do is live all of life in the joy of the message of Easter, the message of grace.

The sawdust in the circle of life reminds us that we are a fallen humanity. In every effort to please God on our own, we trip, fall, and stumble. The cross reminds us that God has come down and reaches out to us because we cannot reach God. Grace means that salvation is God's gift. We only receive it. We do not earn it or deserve it. In Christ we are called by God to live gracefully. The sawdust comes from the small chips that fell from the tree that was cut for the cross of Christ. Through the cross the sawdust now softens the blows of a fallen humanity and holds all the smells of our attempts to make God into our image. Like the clown in the circus we get up again and again and again.

The Christian church has much to gain from beholding the cross from the sawdust circle. Perhaps one of the greatest things the church could learn from clowns and the circus is to look up, laugh, and celebrate life.

Once there was a church that went to a circus to learn how to worship. In the circus there was a man who walked on the very high wire. A beautiful lady kept bowing for the people to applaud. They would have, but their mouths were full of popcorn and their hands held taffy and snow cones. One day they learned to look up. The man on the wire was glad.[6]

In looking up, the people of God might discover that the sacred always takes place in the midst of the secular. What makes

6 Herbert Brokering, *I Opener* (St. Louis, Mo.: Concordia Publishing House, 1974), p. 48.

anything holy is the presence of God. A parking lot, a park, a home, or a workplace can be just as sacred as any church build-

ing, if we learn to look up and behold the cross. Then our lives will become applause to God.

There was a time when I took the whole church staff and their spouses or friends to the circus to learn how to celebrate Epiphany. Very few Protestant churches even have a worship service on Epiphany. This is mainly because Epiphany, January 6, usually does not fall on a Sunday. Some Roman Catholic churches will have a mass on Epiphany, but it is not well attended. Eastern Orthodox Christians know how to celebrate Epiphany. The circus knows how to celebrate Epiphany even though they may not know that they are.

Because I had been a pastor in St. Petersburg, Florida, I knew that Ringling Bros. and Barnum & Bailey always did a whole week of their newest show at the Bayfront Center in St. Petersburg. The Tampa/St. Petersburg area is filled with people who love and support the circus. Most performances were a straw-house, a circus term meaning all the seats were filled. This was still a time of sharpening the acts and the timing of the circus before they went off for a two-year journey. This was also the week in which the television producers brought in their film

crews to film a TV special on The Greatest Show On Earth® that
would be aired later in the year.

This was the time when the audience might see television
and movie comics like Dick Van Dyke or Ernest Borgnine play
the role of a clown or a guest ringmaster. This was also one of the
few times the audience might see either Irvin Feld or his son,
Kenneth, who own and run the great circus, or some of the direc-
tors of the show: Robert MacDougall, the general manager of the
Red Unit; Tim Holst, performance director; the great Antoinette
Concello, the aerial director; or Keith Greene, the music conduc-
tor.[7] The show on Epiphany, January 6, was the time to see the
circus inside out.

Knowing that the Epiphany performance of Ringling Bros.
and Barnum & Bailey Circus is a great learning opportunity, I
purchased tickets for the staff, and their spouses or friends, of St.
John Lutheran Church of Winter Park, Florida, where I was one
of the pastors. The tickets were for the evening performance on
Epiphany, January 6, to the 113th edition of The Greatest Show
On Earth. It was my Christmas gift to them. Epiphany is a great
time to celebrate the gifts of Christmas. So like a bunch of clowns
crowded into a small car we began our journey from Orlando to
St. Petersburg so that we could arrive early enough to watch the
warm-up gags of the clowns. Some of the staff had never been to
a circus. They could not make the connection of the cross and the
sawdust circle. They were excited about going to the circus, but
some of them could not see what this had to do with worship.

Then I realized that it was not just that many of them had not
been to a circus, but also that they did not understand the meaning of Epiphany. So, while traveling to the circus, I shared the
meaning of Epiphany with the staff. They learned that Epiphany
means "to shine forth." It is a razzle-dazzle season of the church
year, beginning with the splendor of the Magi from the East following the bright star of Bethlehem to honor and worship the
newborn king. They brought gifts to honor the king. The season

7 113th Edition Souvenir Program and Magazine of Ringling Bros. and Barnum &
   Bailey Combined Shows, Inc., 1983, pp. 1-2; 37-40; 76-77.

of Epiphany includes the spectacular baptism of Jesus with the descending of the Spirit and the voice from heaven, "You are my Son, the Beloved; with you I am well pleased." There is a focus on the glory of God shown forth in Jesus as he did many miracles. This season concludes with the account of the Transfiguration, where Peter, James, and John saw Jesus standing in dazzling white with Moses and Elijah. Again the voice of God was heard, "This is my Son, the Beloved; with him I am well pleased; listen to him!" Epiphany is a season of "Wow!" And the circus knows how to celebrate it.

On the way to St. Petersburg, I told the staff, "Look for the signs of razzle-dazzle. Look for the star shining forth like the star of Bethlehem. Look for the Wise Men from the East and the gifts from kings to the newborn king. Think of the church liturgy and look for similarities. Look in the secular for the razzle-dazzle of the sacred, the glory of God manifested in Jesus. Watch the faces of the children of all ages and listen to the sounds of the circus: glorious music, the chant of the ringmaster, and the laughter of children." We were pumped for Epiphany!

Upon arriving at the Bayfront Center in St. Petersburg, I encouraged every family to purchase the souvenir program. At that time the cost was $2.50. Even I was surprised from reading the program to discover that the new Epiphany circus of Ringling would feature two of the world's greatest circus stars, both of whom are now dead: the legendary master of mirth, Lou Jacobs, and Gunther Gebel-Williams, the world's most celebrated animal trainer and circus performer. I knew the boss clown of the Red Unit, Wayne Sidley, from previous years when we met at Circus World and he provided instruction for me and for the members of my clown troupe. This was going to be a spectacular show and we would learn so much. And we did!

Before the show began, the clowns worked among the audience. Some stayed on the floor and did walk-a-round along the hippodrome. But many of the clowns went right into the seating area and worked with people. There was laughter all over the

arena as the clowns created relationships with the audience. The
anxiety level of adults and children was reduced with the laughter created by these exalted experts who excelled in exhibiting
exuberance. I turned to the director of music ministry and said,
"It is like worship warm-up, much like when we practice a new
part of the liturgy or a new hymn before the worship service." He
nodded and said, "Ah! I get it!"

The performance director blew his whistle and the clowns
quickly disappeared. The house lights were turned off and everyone was silent. The ringmaster, Dinny McGuire, stepped into the
center ring under the glow of a dozen spot lights and with his
beautiful baritone voice grandly proclaimed, "Ladies and
Gentlemen, Children of All Ages, Ringling Bros. and Barnum &
Bailey Circus proudly presents the 113th edition of The Greatest
Show On Earth!" It was the invocation. He blew his whistle and
suddenly the lights flooded the darkness of the arena and all the
performers and the animals, dressed in spectacular sequined costumes, processed around the hippodrome. The whole arena
sparkled with every color of the rainbow. In came a seemingly
endless stream of horses, camels, elephants, llamas, chim-
panzees, dogs, clowns on stilts, performers from every nation,
and even a tiger riding on the back of an elephant with Gunther
Gebel-Williams! They smiled and waved as the circus band
played the entrance song and the ringmaster sang. They welcomed the audience into the sawdust circle of their lives.

With eyes wide open and with large, smiling faces the audience responded with joy. They were part of the spectacle of
Epiphany. The space had become holy ground. They were ready
for more. "The ringmaster sounds like Pastor Bob," exclaimed
our receptionist, Chris. "He looks as good as Pastor Bob and has
a voice like his!" "How would you like vestments like his, Pastor
Dick?" asked Jerry. I was so excited. The staff—our staff—were
making the connections. Oh, the circus and the church have so
much in common in their traditions. "It is like the procession at
the beginning of worship—crucifer, torchbearers, banner bear-

ers, the choir, and the clergy! The only thing we are missing is the animals!" added Katie, the director of youth and family ministry. Ruth laughed as she said, "Maybe we should use incense!" Pointing to the hippodrome, Doug stated, "Look, it's the Magi on elephants and camels!"

Ringmaster Dinny McGuire introduced each act with dignity and clarity as he kept the circus moving. Like the celebrant in a worship service, he had several costume changes. The colors of his costumes matched a specific theme of a coming act much like the color of the celebrant's chasuble in worship matches the color of the church year or specific saint day. Dinny honored each performer with his voice and this top hat. Together with the circus band and the lighting crew he led the audience from one fantasy to the next. The quality of the performance, the lights, and the colors created a drama that held the audience's attention and wove them into the fantasy to believe they were the performers. Those in the audience were so engaged that it seemed they stopped breathing. Suddenly, at the conclusion of a dramatic fantasy, the house lights came on and in came the clowns to bring the audience back to the reality of life. Act after act the arena was filled with "ooh"s and "aah"s and "ha! ha! ha!"s. Next, about 50 children, guided by members of the circus staff, came from the audience to the hippodrome to participate in the children's spectacle. "Look! It's the children's sermon," shouted Chris joyfully. I responded, "Wait until you see all the work these people do for this one act with children. I am always amazed! They value children being with their families at the circus!" The theme for the children's spectacle was the Pink Panther joins the circus. The bright eyes of every child in the audience were on the 50 other children who were part of the spectacle. It may have been the only time in the circus when 90 percent of the audience was focused on the same act. "Wow! All that work for a few moments with children!" said Andy as he pointed out Lou Jacobs to his wife, Katie.

THINK PINK

Flash, Flair, And Flourish Flanked By Frantic Fanfare Flamboyantly Fill Our Fantastic Forum Of Festival As Practice And Perseverance Promise A Pay-Off For Our Precocious, Prestigious Predator, The Pink Panther, When He Proudly Premieres As Part Of The Particularly Praiseworthy, Panoramically Powerful Precision Pageantry, Precariously Performing: Tantalizing Tumultuous Tumbling Triumphs; Absolutely Astounding Acrobatic Achievements; And Limitless Lion Training Titillations Culminating In A Colossal, Classic Circus Parade Packed With Pachyderms, Crammed With Clowns, Filled With Floats, Studded With Stars And Simply Sizzling With Splendor, Sparkle And Spectacle.

THE PINK PANTHER JOINS
THE GREATEST SHOW ON EARTH[8]

If the circus had ended there, it would have been worth the price of admission. But there was much more to come. The intermission followed the children's spectacle. It was much like the offering time in a worship service—the venders gathering in the money as fast as the ushers in a worship service. Adults prepared their children to participate further in this circus by the purchase of swords that would light up in the dark and flashlights that would whirl the colors of red and blue in the darkness.

During this intermission we stood up and shared the peace and joy of being together in this holy space. It was awesome. Many people, and especially those with children, left their seats and headed for the donikers. That's a circus term for restrooms. The circus has a special language just like the church. The clowns again did their walk-a-rounds and laughter circled the hippodrome. "Hey, Pastor Dick! Look—three rings," exclaimed Doug, "Three rings in the circus. Three rings are the symbol of the Trinity in the church!" Just then the house lights went out.

8 From the 113th Edition Souvenir Program and Magazine, Ringling Bros. and Barnum & Bailey Combined Shows, Inc., 1983, p. 27.

Sword lights and red and blue flashlights shined through the darkened arena. One spotlight focused on the center ring. "Three rings, three crosses—center ring, center cross—major act, Jesus," said Helen, secretary to Pastor Bob. "They are getting it," I thought to myself.

Dinny McGuire's voice introduced the next act, "And now, Ladies and Gentlemen, in the steel cage in the center ring—the world's greatest wild animal trainer, Gunther Gebel-Williams! Watch him as with his voice alone he commands ten Bengal tigers!" This definitely was the main act of the circus. It was amazing. At the close of the act all the tigers but one left the ring to return to their carrying cages. Gunther commanded the tiger to climb up on a platform atop a large mirrored ball. Then he, Gunther, climbed on top of the tiger. The house lights went out and the spot lights only shined upon Gunther, the tiger, and the revolving, mirrored ball. The darkness of the arena was filled with the reflected light from the mirrored ball. It was like seeing thousands of stars in the sky. The entire staff shouted in unison, "Epiphany!" They were seeing the sacred in the secular.

As the acts continued we held our breath and prayed watching the Bauers on the sway poles and the Flying Espanas on the high trapeze. The clowns continued to keep us balanced between fantasy and reality as we moved swiftly toward the final act. All the elephants and all the performers circled the hippodrome for the recessional. The audience stood and applauded as the performers passed by. The band paused for the final blessing of the ringmaster: "Thank you and may all your days be Circus Days!" The band continued to play as the people left the arena. And, all the way back to Orlando, we talked about the wonders of Epiphany that we experienced.

For where two or three are gathered in my name, I am there among them. *(Matthew 18:20)*

The sacred can take place in the secular. That visit to the circus in St. Petersburg was 18 years ago and I still remember the experience vividly. That's what an exciting Epiphany service can do! Beholding the cross from the sawdust circle enables people to see holy moments, holy spaces, holy places, and holy relationships in the midst of daily living.

> Lord, prepare me to be a sanctuary,
> Pure and holy, tried and true;
> With thanksgiving, I'll be a living
> Sanctuary for You.[9]

In my second book that I wrote on clown ministry, *Welcome to the Sawdust Dust Circle Part II: Learning the Art of Clown Ministry*, I designed a game called Holy, Holy, Holy to help people make the connection of the church and the circus, the cross and the sawdust circle. This three-ring game is designed for small groups to discuss and learn of the connections of the church, circus, and daily Christian living. It uses Share Cards, Similarity Cards, Role Playing Cards, and Activity Cards. It is a fun way to share and learn. We can learn so much when we behold the cross from the vantage of the sawdust circle.

9 Words and music of the hymn "Sanctuary" by John Thompson and Randy Scruggs, 1982. Found in *Renew! Songs & Hymns for Blended Worship* (Carol Stream, Ill.: Hope Publishing Co., 1995), #185.

Both the circus and the church have struggled with being true to their belief systems and historical traditions and yet attempting to communicate to a culture that changes more rapidly with each new generation. The marketing question for both the church and the circus is, "How do you reach the audience of the new generations?" This affects architecture as well as program and personnel. After World War II the United States shifted from being primarily agrarian to industrialized. More people moved into the cities where the work was. In the 1950s there was a boom of building churches throughout the cities.

The architecture of the cities brought new designs for church buildings. Buildings of brick, stone, and cement replaced the former white-painted, wooden framed church buildings. The city look replaced the country look. The circus, too, had to make changes at this time. In 1956, John Ringling North, the owner of The Greatest Show On Earth, announced that the circus must change to survive. But it was Irvin Feld's idea to move the circus from the big top daily traveling tent show to extended performances in arenas within larger cities.

> The next afternoon, North telephoned Feld. Six months earlier, Feld had written North a letter telling him that while the era of the gigantic canvas big tops was finished, a new era of arena circuses could begin. Within ten years every major city in American would have a sizable modern amphitheater in which the circus could shine. Moreover, moving the circus indoors would mean

that the old thirty-five-week seasons, at the mercy of
the weather, could give way to forty-six consecutive
weeks, from early January to late November, with six
weeks left over for vacation and rehearsing the new
show, and weather no longer a factor.[10]

As the American culture struggled with integration and with
the role of women in society, so the circus and the church had to
grow through such needed change. History and tradition can
often blind people to the importance and blessings of such
change. It may be that the circus has grown more with the
changes than the church. Some denominations of the Christian
church in the United States have been more successful than others in welcoming and including people of color. Overall those
denominations founded in the United States by white, European
immigrants remain primarily white. In the Evangelical Lutheran
Church in America, of which I am a member, we have had
women clergy only since 1970. Some Christian denominations
still do not have women serving in such roles. It remains a difficult shift from history, traditions, and belief systems.

Although the tradition of the circus was always open to
skilled performers of any nationality, until 1968, when Irvin Feld
hired the King Charles Troupe, there wasn't one African
American in the circus. The incredibly talented young men in this
troupe played basketball while riding unicycles. I remember
watching them for the first time. They were like the Harlem
Globetrotters on wheels. They were wonderful and brought the
same kind of excitement, energy, and joy as did the Globetrotters.
By 1984 Ringling Bros. and Barnum & Bailey Circus had
African American center-ring performers, clowns, showgirls, and
support people. [11]

For a long time women have had active and major roles in

10 From and article "Barnum to Ringling to Feld," by John Culhane, printed in the
113th Edition Souvenir Program and Magazine of Ringling Bros. and Barnum
& Bailey Combined Shows, Inc., 1983, p. 9.

11 John Culhane, *The American Circus* (New York: Henry Holt and Company,
1990), pp. 326-327.

the American circus, but not in the areas of ringmaster or clown. Great women performers have had the center ring in circuses all over the world: Mary Jose Knie and her liberty horses; Ringling's Madam Castello and her horse, Jupiter; the great Miss Cooke on the tight wire in 1842; or Ella Zuila on the high wire in the 1880s; Lillian Leitzel performing on the web; Antoinette Concello, the first woman flyer to do the triple; the Big Apple's Dolly Jacobs on the Roman Rings; Judy Murton doing spins on the trapeze; Mabel Stark, foremost American woman animal trainer; East Germany's Ursula Bottcher and her polar bears; and many more.[12] I remember a time that I saw both a female and a male ringmaster at a performance of Ringling Bros. and Barnum & Bailey Circus. But that did not last more than one year. However, other smaller circuses have had women in the role of ringmaster. In April 2001, I attended the Ashton's Circus in Brisbane, Queensland, Australia. Lorraine (nee Ashton) Grant did an excellent job as the ringmaster for this wonderful family circus.[13]

In 1970, the same year that the branches of Lutherans that now make up the Evangelical Lutheran Church in America allowed women clergy, Ringling Bros. Clown College in Venice, Florida, had seven women in the class. After graduation, two of them were assigned to the traveling units of the show. Peggy Williams was known as First Lady of Clowning because she was assigned to the Red Unit, the first show to get on the road that year. Another female graduate of the class of 1970, Maude Flippen, was assigned to the Blue Unit. Since then there have been many female clowns in both units.[14]

P. T. Barnum once said that "clowns and elephants are the two pegs you hang the circus on."[15] As the culture changed, the circus continued to use many elephants, but the number of

---

12 Howard Loxton, *The Golden Age of the Circus* (New York: Smithmark Publishers, 1997), pp. 38-72.

13 Ashton's Circus is the longest-serving performing arts organization in Australia. It is older than some states and most towns in Australia.

14 John Culhane, *The American Circus* (New York: Henry Holt and Company, 1990), pp. 325-326.

15 George Speaight, *The Book of Clowns* (New York: MacMillan Publishing, Inc., 1980), p. 119.

clowns in the Ringling Bros. and Barnum & Bailey Circus had dwindled from more than one hundred in the late 1930s to only thirteen in the '60s. Many of the remaining clowns were very old. There were even fewer clowns in other circuses. In response to the need, Irvin Feld had a brilliant idea and created Clown College in 1968 to train new clowns for the circuses.

Feld took three of the old clowns and made them the master teachers. The three clowns were Lou Jacobs, an auguste clown; Otto Griebling, a tramp clown; and Bobby Kaye, a whiteface clown. They made up the three basic clown types of the circus.[16] Since then, hundreds of clowns have graduated from Clown College to supply almost every circus in America. However, about two years ago, Kenneth Feld decided to close Clown College. Today, most clowns do not stay with the circus for more than a few years because Clown College had produced an abundance of circus clowns and the yearly pay for a circus clown is very low. Thus there may never be any more great clowns who will clown all their lives, like Mark Anthony, Emmett Kelly, Lou Jacobs, Otto Griebling, and Felix Adler.

Moving into the 21st century has brought new challenges to both the church and the circus. Fewer people of the Boomer and GenXer generations are attending traditional, mainline churches. The next younger generation, the Millennials, have an interest in spirituality but come from homes where no one knows the biblical stories. The Christian church must discover how to reach the new generations with the gospel of Jesus Christ. The form of worship and style of controlled ministries no longer is effective with the younger generations. The culture in the United States has become much more pluralistic. So the challenge is not only reaching the new generations and equipping them to pass on the faith but also for the Christian church to learn how to exist alongside many other forms of religious belief: Islam, Mormon, Buddhism, New Age, and many others. The Christian church

16 John Culhane, *The American Circus* (New York: Henry Holt and Company, 1990), pp. 323-326.

must make a paradigm shift in ministry to focus on a partnership with the home to nurture faith. Many congregations have gone to multiple worship services with a variety of styles. The pipe organ has been replaced by an electronic keyboard as the main instrument for worship. Many congregations have full bands and vocal groups leading worship. Electronic slide shows and videos have joined ciborium and chalice as ecclesiastical language, and projection screens have replaced hymnals. Many congregations have dropped their denominational names from the church signage. Some have tried to target a specific generation. There are great success stories and many failures, but mainline Christian churches know they are losing members. Dr. Merton Strommen and I explain this needed change in our book, *Passing On the Faith: A Radical New Model for Youth and Family Ministry*. The Youth & Family Institute of Augsburg College in Minneapolis, Minnesota, has developed many resources and training programs to assist congregations moving into a new model of ministry.[17]

When the American culture shifted from the industrial age to the information age, the circus had to make many new changes. The high technology of this information age has changed entertainment. It is difficult for the circus to compete with television and movies. Today, many children spend more time watching television than they do being with their parents. Cable television, pay-per-view, satellite dishes, and digital satellite TV offer every type of entertainment in the home at the click of a button. The challenge for the circus to provide something new and to reach the new generations has caused many small family circuses to close. There are fewer circuses in the United States today compared to 50 years ago.

Animal rights people continue to put great pressure on the circuses not to have any animals. Cirque Du Soleil out of Quebec, Canada, has no animals, and has experience great success in reaching a new audience. They use some of the best acro-

17 *Passing On The Faith* and many other resources for strengthening families to nurture faith are available online at www.youthfamilyinstitute.com or by calling the toll-free number 877-239-2492.

batic acts coming out of the Far East and connect it with great technology in a one-ring extravaganza. They even have space on the ground of Walt Disney World® in Orlando, Florida. This European-style contemporary circus plays to sold-out audiences (strawhouse) all over the world. Instead of competing with television, they have won an Emmy Award in special events, Silver Medal at the 32nd New York International Film and TV Festival, and the Ace Award in the variety special category of the National Cable Television Association. Several of their shows are now on video.[18]

The success of Cirque Du Soleil and the challenges of reaching a new audience of the information age empowered Kenneth Feld to develop yet a third circus, but totally different from the Red Unit or the Blue Unit. He created Barnum's Kaleidoscape℠, a one-ring, European-style circus with excellent and comfortable seating in the round. It was designed for much more audience participation and featured David Larible, arguably the greatest performing clown in the world today. The show only had two routines with animals: a flock of trained geese and a liberty horse act, true to the history of the circus. Kaleidoscape played to a strawhouse throughout the United States. I was able to attend one performance of Kaleidoscape and still think it is one of the best entertainment events I have ever seen.

The church and the circus have survived cultural changes in the past. But in the 21st century changes happen more rapidly and in greater number than in past decades. It may be that clown ministry might provide a new symbol and a new presence of the church in the world of the 21st century. It certainly is needed.

Perhaps the many ancient symbols we use today in our worship are all too often archaic and empty echoes of truth. By the time we finish explaining the meaning of the Chi Rho or the Ichthus for the seventeenth time, we need an alarm clock to pick up the worship tempo. We

---

18 *Cirque Du Soleil: We Reinvent the Circus* is one such videotape (New York: PolyGram Video, 1992).

need to have new symbols with a contemporary touch
to communicate the ageless truth that Jesus Christ is
for you.[19]

The clown is more than a symbol that hangs on a wall or is
on the bumper of an automobile. It is more than a button or a
badge informing people that one is a clown even when out of
costume. It is a way of life that points people to Jesus. The clown
as a symbol is more like a stained-glass window: When the light
of the sun shines through the window, people see a story about
God's foolish plan of salvation. Clowns in ministry
are tools to help people see a gracious God who
loves them so much. It is not important to
see the clown. It is important to see God—
to see the cross in the sawdust circle of life.

The clown may be one of the few symbols that can halt the busyness of people of
the 21st century for them to wonder and say,
"Huh?" It may be the best symbol
for an information-age society
because it is one of the few symbols a person can literally put on.
It is a symbol that, when one puts
it on, takes that person deeply into
a theology of the cross. In the theology of the cross a person finds
healing, identity, purpose, hope,
and laughter. The cross brings
renewal, not the clown. The clown
points people to the cross.

You were taught to put away your former way of life,
your old self, corrupt and deluded by its lusts, and to be
renewed in the spirit of your minds, and to clothe your-

19 Bill Paepke, "Clowning in the Church," *Group*, (Loveland, Colo.: Group
Publishing, 1976), December issue, p. 13.

selves with the new self, created according to the likeness of God in true righteousness and holiness.
(Ephesians 4: 22-24)

Clowns in ministry give people a new point of view. They
help people view the sawdust in their lives through the cross of

Christ. Christian clowns create word pictures of the gospel. The word pictures of
the clowns gives people a new angle to
look at one another.

From now on, therefore, we regard
no one from a human point of view;
even though we once knew Christ
from a human point of view, we
know him no longer in that way. So
if anyone is in Christ, there is a new
creation: everything old has passed
away; see, everything has become
new! *(2 Corinthians 5: 16-17)*

Clown ministry has gone up and
down in its popularity in the United
States. That means that people have heard of it, but very few
Christian people have seen it. I think people interpreted the
clown in the church as a novelty rather than a ministry ("It's a
nice way to keep the youth entertained."). Few people thought
that the clown could be a symbol of the presence of God or a tool
for people to see God.

In the late 1960s until the early 1980s clown ministry was at
one of its highest levels of interest in the United States. From the
United States the interest reached into other countries like
Canada, Australia, and the United Kingdom. Much like the circus having a very few great clowns to teach others the history
and art of clowning at Clown College, so Christian clowning had
a few Christ clowns to teach others the art of clown ministry.

In this early time of clown ministry the Rev. Floyd Shaffer
was one of the most influential people. At that time he was a pastor of a Lutheran church in Roseville, Michigan. His major focus
was worship. Because the clown was visual, not dependent upon
words, the clown provided a new angle for Christian people to be
renewed in worship. Shaffer thought the clown should do "divine
interruptions" in worship to create word pictures of what people
are doing throughout the liturgy. Some people thought this was
an intrusion of their comfortable point of view and became
angered at Shaffer's work. But for the most part Shaffer's work
was refreshing and brought much joy. His popularity grew rapidly beyond the Lutheran church to Roman Catholics and to the
Protestants of every denomination and non-denomination.

I have been with Floyd several times,
both to learn and to share. He is an excellent
clown. I think one can learn the most from
Floyd Shaffer by watching Socataco, his
clown character. Socataco is Floyd inside-
out. Socataco can show you clown ministry
better than Floyd can tell you. His work was
so important that Mass Media Ministries
made three films, now in video forms of
Socataco: *The Mark of the Clown*, *A Clown
Is Born*, and *That's Life!* Group Publishing
also used Floyd for a teaching video on
clown ministry. Shaffer provided the church with needed
resources to introduce clown ministry as a legitimate tool for
helping people see the cross in the sawdust circle.

The most powerful vision I have of the work of Floyd Shaffer
is his word picture of the words of institution of the Lord's
Supper in worship. I have never seen it done better. He made the
words of the liturgy that are spoken at every celebration of the
Eucharist, the Lord's Supper, come alive. He provided a new
angle from which I, and others present, could see the holy in the
familiar. To this day, if a clown is used in a congregation to lead

the liturgy of the Eucharist, some part of the mime routine will be of Shaffer's creativity. The clown may not even know that it originated with Floyd Shaffer.

One of the most difficult times Floyd Shaffer had was taking people deeper into the theology of clown ministry. The idea of the clown in ministry and Floyd's popularity grew so rapidly that he simply couldn't keep up with the request to help others begin such an exciting ministry. I remember Floyd telling me many times, "I just don't have time to take people deeper. If I could write about the theology, I would. But I can't, so I will simply do it!"

Nick Weber was another person who was very influential in clown ministry in 1971 to the early 1980s. This former Jesuit priest ran one of the smallest traveling circuses in the United States, the Royal Lichtenstein & One-Quarter-Ring Circus. Nick and his troupe traveled throughout the country and he was especially popular on college campuses. Much like the court jester, Nick's clowning was very satirical and gave a different point of view from which to see what is truly happening in our nation and in the world. This brought joy to some and inflamed others.

The Royal Lichtenstein & One-Quarter-Ring Circus was like having a Renaissance festival in a neighborhood park, or even

someone's back yard. Children and adults were pleased and fascinated to discover that Nick and his troupe used more common animals like cats, dogs, birds, a miniature horse, and a monkey. Nick was always playful. He believed that play could lead to prayer.[20] I remember being with Nick at one of the early clown ministry conferences of the Christian Clown

20 Cal Samara, *The Joyful Christ: The Healing Power of Humor*, (San Francisco: Harper & Row Publishers, 1986), p. 45.

Connection in Orlando, Florida. In the evening, after the partici-
pants had seen the Royal Lichtenstein & One-Quarter-Ring
Circus, Nick spoke to the group of excited clowns. Most did not
understand him and some didn't like him. He gave them a different point of view from which to look at their own clown ministries. Much like his clowning in the circus, he was highly critical. I remember the key phrases that cut at some people, but
opened others like me to see ministry in a new way: "Clowns in
ministry aren't into conversion and handing out tracts, pam-
phlets, or even Bibles. The Christological question is not, 'Are
you saved?'" His challenge went even deeper when he said, "Far
too many clowns in ministry have such a narrow Christology that
they have no theology!" Some were angered at his statement and
with great heartburn said, "Humph!" Most did not have a clue of
what he was saying. But I remember listening to the words of that
rebel Roman Catholic priest and saying, "Wow!" He gave me a
whole new angle to view my clown ministry and myself.

In 1983, the Rev. Bill Peckham of Springfield, Illinois,
organized an ecumenical group of Christian clowns, The Holy
Fools. Bill was a United Methodist pastor. This organization was
made up of members from 37 Christian denominations. Bill esti-
mated that about 4000 people were known to be involved in
clown ministry at that time and perhaps thousands of others
unknown. The emphasis of Bill's teaching was more on finding
the clown within a person and not being afraid to be a fool for
Christ. Many of the Holy Fools visited hospitals and mental insti-
tutions.

Peckham himself began his clown ministry by dressing up as
a clown and visiting a nursing home. The first man he visited
there, much to his surprise, was blind. Clown ministry is visual,
and logically will not be effective with those who cannot see.
Peckham was even more surprised when the blind man expressed
that he always wanted to see a clown, then lightly touched the
clown's wig, face, and costume. The blind man said he felt so
blessed—it was the first time he had ever seen a clown. Tears ran

down Peckham's face. Healing took place. Neither man could figure out who should thank whom.

The power of clown ministry gave Peckham a new angle to assess his own ministry. He moved into a new style of crisis intervention ministry. Being a clown has given Peckham a new angle to bring forgiveness, love, hope, and wholeness to people who are fractured and out of breath. Cal Samara in *The Joyful Christ* quotes Peckham to say:

> The clown has been a universally loved symbol of hope, happiness, and just plain fun. Whether appearing as a circus clown or as Charlie Chaplin's little tramp or Red Skelton's buffoon, the clown is vulnerable, attracts rejection and hurts, is the butt of jokes and pranks, and gets the worst end of every deal. Clowns are forever falling down but always getting up, brushing themselves off, smiling, and trying again. They are never fully defeated. They never give up. They embody hope and joy in the face of adversity.[21]

As a result of the rise of clown ministry in Christian churches throughout the United States in the 1970s, John Luoma wrote an article called "The Emergence of the Clown," concerning the rediscovery of the clown as an important symbol for the Christian church:

> In the light of the last few years, one might…claim that not only is he [the clown] reappearing on the stage, he is also becoming part of the religious life of the churches.[22]

With the growth of technology and information-giving in the late 1980s until now, most leaders of the Christian church became so busy playing catch-up so they could communicate the

21 Cal Samara, *The Joyful Christ: The Healing Power of Humor*, (San Francisco: Harper & Row Publishers, 1986), pp. 41-44.
22 John K. Luoma, "The Emergence of the Clown," *The Cresset*, (Valparaiso, Ind.: University Faculty, 1977), November/December issue.

gospel message to highly technical people, that they did not notice that many, many congregations had stopped growing. There were fewer baptisms of children and adults being recorded. Average worship attendance had been dropping regularly. Very few adults went to Bible classes or Christian life classes. It became more difficult to find people who had the faith and the time to teach other adults and their children. Very few people talked about God outside the space of the church buildings. Few families were connecting to Christian congregations. High technology brought a low touch of relationships.

Research has shown that more people are living now at a distance from one another within the same household. Many parents do not know their children, and children do not know their parents. We live in a culture that loves children, but doesn't value them. If parents and other adults valued children, they would spend more time together laughing and playing. In this age of people locked in technology, building virtual relationships through computers, looking for a quick-fix pill to heal dis-ease, and using dollars and material things to shorten distance in relationships, maybe it is time for the clown to emerge again.

> "The paradox of the clown appears in various ways throughout history," says Shaffer. "It seems to be an apocalyptic symbol that appears in times of hopelessness. Maybe clowns are raised at these moments in history as reminders that God is alive and well and continuing to work in the world."[23]

The Christian church in the 21st century needs the clown to prophetically emerge and speak forth God's foolish message of love to a world that is so busy and preoccupied with itself that it doesn't want to hear. The clown can create word pictures of the real presence of a God of love to a nation of people wearing

---

23 Cal Samara, *The Joyful Christ: The Healing Power of Humor*, (San Francisco: Harper & Row Publishers, 1985), p. 46.

headphones and cell phones. The clown can make people rushing by to stop, behold, and wonder again.

I have seen the Holy Spirit work through the symbol of the clown for the past 30 years that I have been active in clown ministry. The need for the emergence of the symbol of the clown became so evident to me during our last clown ministry pilgrimage to eastern Europe in the summer of 2001. I had accepted an invitation to bring the clowns to assist with an Evangelical Faith Festival and Christian Children's Crusade near Salmopol, Poland. I joined Herb Brokering and Penne Sewall as leaders of this pilgrimage. This was a pilgrimage, not a mission trip. The focus

was not on what we, as clowns, would do for other people. Rather, the focus of this clown ministry pilgrimage was for each clown to find holy ground where God would strengthen each or our relationships with God and with one another. On this pilgrimage the cross in the sawdust circle would give each of us an new angle to behold

our identity, relationships, and responsibilities of living life close to God through Jesus Christ. We were sent by God to be healed ourselves.

We learned to move slowly in clown ministry, to wait for the people to invite the clowns to take the next step. The angle of the cross in the sawdust circle gave us new insights as to how to connect to children of all ages in a land in which we did not know the spoken language. We learned to be gentle, unassuming, and even inconspicuous as we approached people. From this angle we were reminded that the only thing that is important is to be transparent so that the people saw Christ. We came armed with many things to give away and learned that it is the relationships that count. We were the receivers.

Clowning before a strawhouse of children under a huge tent
and more than 2000 adults renewed our calling to be fools for
Christ. The smiles, expressions of joy, and laughter of the children
of all ages brought a breath of fresh air to each of us. God had
taken the rain and the mud of that place and made it into a holy
celebration of people who want to grow deeply
into a relationship with God. From
the symbol of the clown, both the
audience and the clowns, saw
and participated in the love of
God. It was a festival of the
children of all ages playing,
"Tag, You're It!" with the
gospel. We learned that there
is an "a-ha!" in every "ha! ha!"

Elderly women who lived together in a retirement home of
the Evangelical Church in Poland were surprised when they saw
their beloved bishop bringing a bunch of clowns to visit them. It
was like bringing each of them a bouquet of flowers. They
responded with joy and laugher at clearly seeing the word-pic-
tures of the gospel made by the clowns.

At the Emaus House (they spell it with only one *M*), not too
far from Bielsko Biala, elderly people who for more than a
month had not been able to leave their beds because of pain,

filled the chapel to be with the clowns. Some remember our first visit in 1991. Others had been told the story of the church clowns who share the healing gospel of Jesus Christ. They laughed and we laughed so hard that tears filled our eyes. The nurses were pleased and the people were

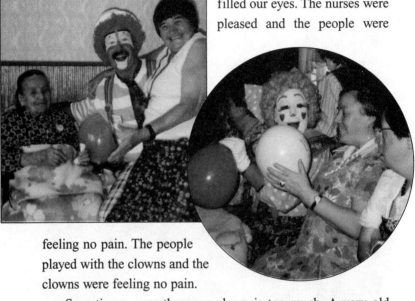

feeling no pain. The people played with the clowns and the clowns were feeling no pain.

Sometimes more than one clown is too much. A very old woman cried out in fear several times. The nurses did not understand and finally removed her from the chapel to the quiet of the hallway close to her room. But one of the clowns, Lesley, looked at the woman from the angle of the cross in the sawdust circle and went to the woman by herself. As I looked down the hallway I saw this wonderful high-school-aged clown kneeling beside the wheelchair of a very old and dear woman. The woman reached out her hand, touched the clown's face, and brought the two of them together cheek to cheek. They played "Tag, You're It!" and Jesus smiled and laughed with them.

An elderly man who missed the clowns in the chapel was awakened only to see the beautiful whiteface of Wobnair, clown and my dear friend, Penne Sewall. The man did not know what to make of this new symbol for the church. He was the father of two sons who became bishops of the church. We had tea together; his wife joined us. The clowns were transparent and all the man saw was Jesus. He and his wife shared their faith stories with the clowns. They sang their faith and we wept. This elderly man took pilgrim clowns deep, deep into faith. "I will see you next time in heaven!" he exclaimed. He only saw Jesus and we saw one of the saints of the church.

I saw tears cascade from the eyes down the cheeks of the senior pastor, vulnerably standing before his congregation in worship, as Wobnair included him in the making of the cross and the passing on of the blessing of God. This very simple move-ment of a clown and a pastor joining a finger to make a cross gave this pastor a new angle from which to see his ministry. His joy grew even more when he saw the faces of many of his peo-ple—faces with a hundred wrinkles weathered by the harshness of life under past communism—break forth with deep laughter. He saw the new life of the gospel in his beloved people.

Seeing all of these events, Bishop Anweiler, the regional bishop of the Evangelical Church of Poland in the area of Bielsko Biala stated, "I want to be the first clown bishop of the church in Poland!" We all laughed and thought to ourselves, "He already is!" The cross in the sawdust circle gave us another angle to look at even the ministry of a bishop. How he loved and cared for the people of Poland! The pilgrim clowns learned about servanthood in ministry.

The symbol of the clown brought new meaning to us all. Even my mentor and friend, Herb Brokering, who is the most creative person of God I have ever met, gained new insights into theology by looking through the cross in the sawdust circle. He saw the hobo clown as suffering clown of the cross, the whiteface clown as the Easter clown, the joy-bringer, and the auguste clown as the Epiphany clown, the one who searches and beholds. He couldn't stop thinking about it, talking about it, or writing about it. He affirmed all the clowns and encouraged them to do more and learn more.

The symbol of the clown helps people of different nations see what is already there in a different light. The clown can bring new meaning to things that are very old. In Wittenberg, Germany, also known as Lutherstadt, the clowns joined hands and stretched across the city square to join two statues together of the great reformers Martin Luther and Philip Melanchton. The clowns created a new vision to see the two statues that have been there for hundreds of years in a new way. No one in Wittenberg that day had gathered to look at the statues. Busy people just rushed by. Suddenly people stopped and a crowd gathered. People grabbed for their cameras. This was a new picture. "I get it! They're friends!" exclaimed one man. Others asked about the identity of the statues, the stories of the statues, who were the clowns, and what was happening. Previous to the action of the clowns, these busy people were not aware of such a connection and were not talking with one another. Now the discussions went on long after the clowns had moved on.

All day long in Wittenberg the clowns connected history with faith. They gave new vision to what has been in the town for

ages. By one of the corners of the *Stadtkirche* (city church), between the church and the chapel, the clowns gathered for another word picture. Some clowns placed themselves carefully in an evergreen tree, much like Christmas ornaments. But these clowns were sad and began to weep. The tree looked like it has been weeping all its evergreen life because of what it saw. High in the corner, near the roof of this church building built before Martin Luther is a painful and hurtful symbol of Jewish people sucking from a pig. It is a sad picture and an indictment of the Christian church. Most visitors to Wittenberg do not even know it is there. In 1996 the local people placed a large bronze plaque symbolizing that this wound has not been healed. It was placed flush on the ground amongst the cobblestones. Still, few people see it or understand it. But the clowns weeping with the tree pointed to a new picture right in front of the plaque. Two clowns dressed in nurses' garb were trying to patch up wounds in a hobo clown, posed as Christ on the cross. Upon seeing the clowns, a local man, told others, "This has never been done in this town before!" Soon others gathered and saw old things in a new way. It caused them to wonder and talk with one another.

I think the clown can be an effective tool of the church as it communicates the gospel of Jesus Christ to children of all ages and of many nations. The church needs this new symbol as it grows in the 21st century. But the clown cannot be just a symbol that hangs on the wall or is displayed on someone's car bumper. My deepest concern is that clowns must be well trained in ministry in a theology of the cross. This must be a ministry, not a novelty. Dr. Heije Faber, former professor of psychology of religion and pastoral psychology at the University of Tilburg in the Netherlands makes a similar statement as he compares a minister to the work of a circus clown:

> In my book, Pastoral Care in the Modern Hospital, I compare the minister, working among medical specialists, with a clown in a circus, who works among the men on the flying trapeze and the tamers of lions and tigers. I said that the clown makes the circus human, because he—metaphorically speaking—has contact with the spectators on a wave length of his own. I added that one must be careful not to see in the clown a kind of dilettante; he is not, his act must be trained. The clown, too, is a professional.[24]

24 Heije Faber, "Second Thoughts on the Minister as a Clown," *Pastoral Psychology*, (Human Sciences Press, 1979), Volume 28, Winter.

Thus, the purpose of my writing this book is to provide a solid, biblical theology of clown ministry so that Christian clowns can be well trained for an effective ministry in the 21st century.

The Clod and the Breath of God

We believe in the Holy Spirit, the Lord, the giver of life...[1]

What gives life? This important question of people of any country, of any age, of any century is also at the heart of a theology of clown ministry. Daily newspapers in every community are filled with story after story about a different question: What takes life? So every day we read about murders, floods, tornadoes, fires, earthquakes, hurricanes, disease, hail, lightning, automobile accidents, financial loss, bankruptcy, and many other personal and community disasters. But rarely does the news focus on the question "What gives life?"

Perhaps the reason that the question "What gives life?" does not make the news and isn't a popular question is because that question brings a person into theological discussion. This question is a discussion about God. The present culture in the United States has separated church and state to such an extreme that God is not seen in the everyday life of an individual. Individual rights has been stressed so much that there is no sense of community. If anything, wealth has been expressed by our culture as the key to really living. Thus there is no need for a message of a total

---

1 The Nicene Creed from *Lutheran Book of Worship*, (Minneapolis: Augsburg Publishing House) 1978, p. 64. The Nicene Creed is one of the three ecumenical creeds accepted by the Christian church first in 325 A.D. at the Council of Nicaea to give a clear stance against the Arian heresy. Later, in 381 A.D., at the Council of Constantinople, minor changes were made and it was reaffirmed as a confession of the Christian Church at the Council of Chalcedon in 451 A.D.

dependency on God. The cultural message is that we can build life and live life totally on our own.

Yet in the midst of a culture of materialism, individualism, and narcissism, death still raises the question "What gives life?" There must be more to life than focusing on oneself. People with everything still say they are searching for something that brings meaning and purpose to their lives. No matter what the cultural message, the effects of sin still touch us all. No matter what our status, we all die. So even the disaster, destruction, and death stories of the media continue to raise the question "What gives life?"

The Holy Scriptures and the confessions of the Christian church point to God as the source of life and the purpose of life to live in a holy relationship with the Creator. To be created in the image of God (*imago dei*) gives the creation the purpose of imaging God to all of creation.

The point of the creation story is to point to the glory of God—"In the beginning God.…" The purpose of life is to live in a right relationship with God in a way that always points to the glory of God. The creation story clearly shows the difference between the Creator and the creation. Life is totally dependent on God, not oneself.

> In the beginning when God created the heavens and the earth, the earth was a formless void and darkness covered the face of the deep, while a wind from God swept over the face of the waters. Then God said.…"
> (*Genesis 1:1-3*)

God used water, word, and wind or breath in the creation. God spoke God's word and the chaos was ordered and the formless took form. Everything was created just as God had envisioned and spoken. It was created good, i.e., in a right relationship with the creator.

> God saw everything that he had made, and indeed, it was very good. (*Genesis 1:31*)

In chapter two of Genesis we are given a unique description
of how God made human beings:

> Then the Lord God formed man from the dust of the
> ground, and breathed into his nostrils the breath of life;
> and the man became a living being. *(Genesis 2:7)*

I love this story—it not only answers what gives life, but also
show the unique relationship human beings have with God and
all of God's creation. From the dust, the dirt, the earth, God created human beings. God took a clod, gave it shape, and breathed
the creative wind, God's breath, into the nostrils of Adam, the
man. The Hebrew word used in this scripture for breath or wind
is *ruach*. It is a playful, powerful word. In pronouncing it, it
sounds like God threw up—RUACH! Full of God's breath, the
man, Adam, became a living being. Wow! What gives life? The
breath of God, the wind of God, the Holy Spirit gives life to
human beings. To be alive is to be filled with the breath of God.
To live is to live in a relationship with the Creator God.

Human beings are the only creation of God with the breath
of God. Human beings were created to live close to the earth,
close to all of God's creation.

> The Lord God took the man and put him in the
> garden of Eden to till it and keep it. *(Genesis 2:15)*

The word *clown* is a 16th-century English word meaning
"clod," "clot," or "clump." In most all languages *clown* means
rustic, one who is close to the earth, a boor, or relating to the
fields. According to Genesis 1 and 2, is that not what we all
are—clods? We are clods with the breath of God, created to live
close to God and close to God's creation. The clown reminds us
that all human beings are clods.

But the story in Genesis 3 is how sin knocked the wind, the
ruach, out the human beings. Without the breath of God all
things die, including human beings.

When you hide your face, they are dismayed; when you
take away their breath, they die and return to their dust.
When you send forth your spirit [or breath], they are
created; and you renew the face of the ground.
(Psalm 104:29, 30)

By the sweat of your face you shall eat bread until you
return to the ground, for out of it you were taken; you
are dust, and to dust you shall return. *(Genesis 3:19)*

Without the breath of God, we are left to our own frailties.
All in God's creation are affected by sin. We can no longer live
in close relationship with all of creation. There is discord, distance, disease, destruction, and death. Human beings live in fear
instead of in love, apart from instead of a part of, and for themselves instead of for God and for all creation. Instead of walking
in a right relationship with God, sin now causes humankind to
trip, fall, and stumble. There is nothing the creation can do to
restore its relationship with the creator.

Creator God does not stay at a distance and simply judge the
fallen action of humankind. Rather, God has a plan to give
mouth-to-mouth resuscitation to humankind who are out of
breath. God stoops down, in Jesus, the Christ, and gives us the
breath of God. Through the life, death, resurrection, and ascension of Jesus, God redeems, renews, and restores us. Through
Jesus, the Christ, we receive the breath of God. We are given life
again to live in a relationship with God. We are totally dependent
on the grace of God. Renewed and restored through Christ, we
can again live in a right relationship with God to the praise and
glory of the Creator, redeemer, and sanctifier God.

...just as he [God] chose us in Christ before the foundation of the world to be holy and blameless before him in
love. He destined us for adoption as his children through
Jesus Christ, according to the good pleasure of his will,
to the praise of his glorious grace that he freely

bestowed on us in the Beloved. In him we have redemption through his blood, the forgiveness of our trespass-
es, according to the riches of his grace that he lavished
on us. With all wisdom and insight he has made known
to us the mystery of his will, according to his good
pleasure that he set forth in Christ, as a plan for the fullness of time, to gather up all things in him, things in
heaven and things on earth. In Christ, we also obtained
an inheritance, having been destined according to the
purpose of him who accomplishes all things according
to his counsel and will, so that we, who were the first to
set our hope on Christ, might live for the praise of his
glory. In him you also, when you had heard the word of
truth, the gospel of your salvation, and had believed in
him, were marked with the seal of the promised Holy
Spirit; this is the pledge of our inheritance toward
redemption as God's own people, to the praise of his
glory. *(Ephesians 1:4-14)*

The clown serves as a reminder of our humanity, of how frail
we are, and of our total dependence on God. Throughout the ages
and among many cultures, the clown has helped people look at
themselves and wonder about life and what gives life. In our
present culture even people connected to the Christian church
become so trapped in the seriousness of lives that demand perfection, that they cannot laugh at their own weaknesses. In fact,
they spend all their lives trying not to die and to hide their human
natures. Such seriousness of trying to do everything perfectly
distorts our theology. Our theology claims that God has
redeemed and restored everything by grace. Our striving does not
change our fallen state nor does it bring us a breath of fresh air.
God brings us that holy breath through Jesus Christ. We simply
are called to live in the grace of God. Sandwiched between two
shepherd stories, Jesus says in John 10:10:

I came that they may have life, and have it abundantly.

Because it is so easy to get trapped in perfectionism, every community and every culture needs clowns to remind them of their humanity and the difference between the creator and the creation. The clown was used in most cultures to remind people of the reality of human nature.

The first dramas performed by humans were done not as entertainment, but as forms of ritual. Primitive men believed that through dramatic enactments symbolizing the seasonal cycle, the hunt or the harvest, they could perform a kind of sympathetic magic and so gain the benevolence of the forces of nature. Yet an element of foolery and caricature often intruded into most sacred rites. Man seems to have instinctively recognized a need to exorcise some of the awe of the ritual mystery through comedy.[2]

Similar clown-like figures appear among the Hopi Indians of New Mexico, the folk theatres of Greece, the court jesters of Europe, the stage clowns of the 16th century, the great clowns of the silent movies of the early 20th century, and the circus clowns of today.

Stock characters, whose names may change but whose function is clear, also crop up in everyday play. There is the bald-headed fool, the old fool, the fat fool, the fool with warts on his face. In the Atellan Farce there is Bucco, the comic slave; Maccus, the country bumpkin; Pappus, the old dotard; Dosennus, the sharp tongue hunchback; Manducus, grinding his teeth and frightening the children. Although the plays vanished these personalities are with us still. They are the universal clowns.[3]

So the great clowns of our culture inform us of our humanity and give us permission to laugh at ourselves. We trip, we fall, and we make mistakes. We are certain that we are right even when proven wrong. We cover up our weaknesses so that others only see our strengths. We cannot let people know us inside-out.

---

2 George Speaight, *The Book of Clowns* (New York: MacMillan Publishing Co., 1980), p. 4.

3 George Speaight, *The Book of Clowns*, p. 6.

We are too frightened to laugh. From the wit of Wil Rogers, the
pantomime of Red Skelton; the slapstick of Buster Keaton and
Charlie Chaplin; the antics of Lucille Ball; the monologues of
Johnny Carson, Jay Leno, Arsenio Hall, David Letterman, and
many more, we are given a reminder of our humanity and permission to laugh at ourselves. It is all for the health of society.

Because the clowns are "of the earth" and live close to the
earth, the role they play in the circus is to bring the audience back
to earth, back to reality from the fantasy of the performers.
Because of the exaggerated made-up faces and the brightly col-
ored costumes, the clowns appear to be the least likely members
of the circus to connect to the reality of life. But in fact they are
the human element of the circus.

A mystique of the circus is weaving the audience into the
fantasies of the circus performers. The ringmaster, with the aid of
the lighting crew and the circus band, draws attention to the performers with the hope that the audience will identify with them
during the act.

Imagine:

> Ringmaster Harold Ronk makes an eloquent gesture
> with his gloved hand. "Just back from a sen-sa-tional
> tour of Europe," his big voice echos, "please welcome
> the Greatest Show On Earth—the First Family of the Air!
> The Flying Gaonas!"[4]

The band begins to play a Strauss waltz and the spotlights
follow the members of the flying family as they climb up the lad-
der to the flying apparatus. Slowly the total attention of members
of the audience is drawn from reality to the fantasy of the performers as they each do a practice flight from the bar to the hands
of the catcher and back. All eyes and emotions are captured high
over ring number two. Suddenly the music stops and only one
spotlight shines on a handsome young Mexican man. Everyone

---

4 Tito Gaona with Harry L. Graham, *Born to Fly* (Los Angeles: Wild Rose, 1984),
   p. 30.

is quiet. The audience is drawn into the fantasy that each is truly this performer.

> "Over ring two," the ringmaster announces dramatically, "the amazing young Mexican flier—Tito Gaona—will attempt the most difficult and dangerous trick of all. The triple somersault—to the hands of the catcher!" Then in a lower voice, he adds, "Watch him!"[5]

The audience is caught in the fantasy. Those watching hold their breath during this death-defying act. Because they are so focused high above ring number two, some miss their mouths as they continue to eat popcorn. For just this very short time everyone identifies with Tito Gaona. They draw a breath, gasp, and hold the breath, "Wooop!" as Tito flies and turns. They emotionally reach out with Tito's arms to the strong arms of the catcher. They have said prayers! It all happens so fast. The arms connect and Tito returns to the apparatus, stands tall, grabs the support wire, smiles, extends his free arm in triumph to the crowd and gives the audience permission to breath again. The excitement of the audience is as high as the performer. They all exhale, "Aaah! We made it!" They applaud their great feat!

Those who design a circus know that an audience cannot endure going from one extreme fantasy to the next. They must bring them back down to earth after being caught in a fantasy. How is that done? They use the only human element of the circus, the clowns, to bring them back to earth. With the sound of the ringmaster's whistle, the music changes, on come the house lights, and in comes a bundling bunch of buffoonery. In the middle of the arena, prankster passengers pack a laughable load of mixed-up merriment into a silly-looking sedan, with dozens of denizens creating carefree comedy. The audience relaxes from the intensity of the fantasy into a laughter of reality. The members of the audience remember when they also had packed too

5 Tito Gaona with Harry L. Graham, *Born to Fly*, p. 30.

many people into a Pontiac. They remember when they took enough luggage for three weeks on a simple weekend outing. The clowns exaggerate simple human acts to give the audience permission to laugh at themselves.

> Stupid and illogical actions produce laughs, at least when performed by a good clown. The clown's ability to evoke feelings of superiority in the spectator plays a hidden role in all of clowning.[6]

The clowns' tremendous amount of misguided energy and exaggerated motions, which seemingly accomplish very little, remind the audience of other events in their own lives and frees them to laugh. They have been brought from the fantasy of the spectacular back to the reality of life on earth. Laughter is the sign of the transition.

The clown is the bridge or the link between fantasy and reality. The clown is the only one of the members of the circus who touch the people. Before a circus performance begins, the clowns are among the audience, warming them up and preparing them for the coming emotional roller coaster of the circus. The clown's laughter is the audience's.[7] The clown is well aware that she or he comes from the earth and lives close to the earth. The clown does not put down a person, but rather lowers him- or herself to give the person in the audience a superior vision. The clown is a sign of hope for the audience. Despite the problems confronted in the routine, the clown keeps on going. Blown-up, shrunken, fooled, foiled, tricked, tread upon, and chased after, the clown always gets up and endures.

John H. Towsen describes this well as he writes of Emmett Kelly:

> Kelly's "Weary Willie" is a sad fellow—even more so than Chaplin's tramp—who never talks and never

6 John Towsen, *Clowns* (New York: Hawthorn Books, Inc., 1976), p. 206.
7 John Towsen, *Clowns*, pp. 58-59.

cracks a smile. His failure to accomplish simple tasks, much less to be as talented as the other circus performers, is cause for sympathetic laughter and not derision.[8]

The Christ clown or church clown is not only aware of humanity, but also believes that the Creator God has stooped down in Jesus Christ to redeem and renew all of humankind. That is why the Christ clown continues to move forward in life despite the problems. The Christ clown also calls other people who struggle with life to move forward with hope. In Christ, God restores the life-giving breath of the Holy Spirit and the hope of a life forever in the presence of God. St. Paul describes the role of the Christ clown in Roman 5:1-5:

> Therefore, since we are justified by faith, we have peace with God through our Lord Jesus Christ, through whom we have obtained access to this grace in which we stand; and we boast in our hope of sharing the glory of God. And not only that, but we also boast in our sufferings, knowing that suffering produces endurance, and endurance produces character, and character produces hope, and hope does not disappoint us, because God's love has been poured into our hearts through the Holy Spirit that has been given to us.

The clown interrupts in the middle of some acts of the circus and in the middle of life to remind people of their humanity. People laugh as a sign of remembering.

The Vulnerability of the Clown

The clown constantly takes the risk of being vulnerable. It is only in exposing his or her weaknesses that the clown makes people feel free to laugh at authentic humanity. One definition of a clown I use in teaching is that a clown is one who lives life

8 John Towsen, *Clowns*, p. 296.

inside-out. Many people are afraid that if others knew them inside-out, they would not be loved by them. So those people keep their distance from others and live so that no one knows what is really going on inside. The sadness of this lifestyle is that such people will never know that they are loved for who they are. They never take the risk to be vulnerable and expose others to their weaknesses as well as their strengths.

But the true clown knows that there is a price to pay in exposing one's humanity. The true clown takes what many hide in the inside, and lives life inside-out so that everyone can see who she is. Clowns share their weaknesses, faults, mistakes, sinful nature, but also share their faith in a gracious, forgiving God. The Christ clown knows that the price for humanity has been paid in full in God's action in Christ.

> When Jesus had received the wine, he said, "It is finished." Then he bowed his head and gave up his spirit. *(John 19:30)* [9]

In his explanation of the second article of the Apostles' Creed, the reformer Dr. Martin Luther shows why a person can now live life inside-out by describing the price that was paid for the redemption of all people.

What does this mean?

Answer: I believe that Jesus Christ, true God, begotten of the Father from eternity, and also true man, born of the virgin Mary, is my Lord, who has redeemed me, a lost and condemned creature, delivered me and freed me from all sins, from death, and from the power of the devil, not with silver and gold but with his holy and precious blood and with his innocent sufferings and death,

9 The New Testament Greek word for "it is finished," is *tetelistai*, the perfect passive of *teleo*. It means that the sacrifice was paid in full, it was totally completed. See *Theological Dictionary of the New Testament*, edited by Gerhard Kittel and Gerhard Friedrich, translated by Goeffrey W. Bromily (Grand Rapids, Michigan: Wm. B Eerdmans Publishing Co, 1972), Volume VIII, pp. 57-61.

in order that I may be his, live under him in his kingdom, and serve him in everlasting righteousness, innocence, and blessedness, even as he is risen from the
dead and lives and reigns to all eternity. This is most certainly true.[10]

The clown reminds us that because the price has been paid
for our fallen humanity we can go on. In Christ we are forgiven.
We are free to fail. We can learn from our failures. In a culture
that clamors for success at all cost, forces a person to hide feelings, and promotes the belief that money is power, the clown is a
symbol of a counterculture. The Christ clown can live life inside-
out because Christ has turned the world upside down:

> Blessed are the poor in spirit, for theirs is the kingdom
> of heaven. Blessed are those who mourn, for they will
> be comforted. Blessed are the meek, for they will inherit
> the earth. Blessed are those who hunger and thirst for
> righteousness, for they will be filled. Blessed are the
> merciful, for they will receive mercy. Blessed are the
> pure in heart, for they will see God. Blessed are the
> peacemakers, for they will be called children of God.
> Blessed are those who are persecuted for righteousness'
> sake, for theirs is the kingdom of heaven. Blessed are
> you when people revile you and persecute you and utter
> all kinds of evil against you falsely on my account.
> Rejoice and be glad, for your reward is great in heaven,
> for in the same way they persecuted the prophets who
> were before you. *(Matthew 5: 3-12)*

Because Christ has turned the world upside-down the Christ
clown does not have to be afraid to show weakness. The weakness can be used by God to show strength. So the clown knows

10 Book of Concord translated by Theodore G. Tappert (St. Louis, Mo.: Concordia
Publishing House, 1959), p. 345. The Book of Concord of 1580 contains
Luther's Small Catechism printed in 1529.

it is more important to be underwhelming than overwhelming. In
2 Corinthians 12:7-10 St. Paul writes about this difficult lesson
he learned:

> Therefore, to keep me from being too elated, a thorn
> was given me in the flesh, a messenger of Satan to tor-
> ment me, to keep me from being too elated. Three times
> I appealed to the Lord about this, that it would leave
> me, but he said to me, "My grace is sufficient for you,
> for power is made perfect in weakness." So I will boast
> all the more gladly of my weaknesses, so that the power
> of Christ may dwell in me. Therefore I am content with
> weaknesses, insults, hardships, persecutions, and calami-
> ties for the sake of Christ; for whenever I am weak, then
> I am strong.

Some people think that clowns are only for laughter, joy, and
celebration. But because the clown is of the earth and lives close
to the earth, the clown can also plant tears. The clown is vulnerable and risks living life inside-out by showing deep feelings of
pain and loss. Jesus gave a new law—that we love one another:

> This is my commandment, that you love one another as I
> have loved you. No one has greater love than this, to lay
> down one's life for one's friends. *(John 15:12, 13)*

To live in this love is to be vulnerable to the pain of those
who abuse it. Because clowns live close to the earth of a fallen
world they will experience pain and suffering. They will see the
inhumanity of humankind. There is more to life than just laughing. In growing through life one experiences both tragedy and
comedy, sadness and joy, tears and laughter. Tears and laughter
share a common source. Clowns will plant tears—their own and
the tears of others.

At the time that I am writing this book I have made four
clown ministry pilgrimages to eastern Europe. Joined with me as

leaders of such clown ministry pilgrimages were the Dr. Herbert Brokering, the most creative person I have ever met, and Penne Sewall, a fellow Christ clown teacher. Herb was a leader on all four pilgrimages; Penne, the last two. On each pilgrimage we visited one of the death camps, not dressed as clowns, but as vulnerable lovers who live life inside-out. We visited Buchenwald, Auschwitz, and Birkenau. Cascades of tears rolled from our eyes down our cheeks to the very ground where this evil took place. Even the birds did not sing. Living close to the earth only brought more tears as we saw, felt, and learned of more details of this holocaust. It was more painful than any of us could endure alone. Like Adam and Eve, our eyes were opened to good and evil and we knew the difference between the Creator God and creation. We planted prayers of tears for those who died, who endured, and for ourselves. In our vulnerability we were fully reminded of our total dependency on God. We grew deeper in our understanding of the ministry of a clown. We continue to weep daily.

Roly Bain, an Anglican priest and wonderfully talented clown from England expresses:

> But true clowning is costly. It is costly because it is founded upon vulnerability and playfulness, and the best clowns are those who can not only play quite openly in all their vulnerability, but who can also play with their vulnerability too. It's the vulnerability of lovers who are able simply to be themselves with each other because of their love. It's the vulnerability of children in their readiness to do anything, accept anyone, and know nothing of fear. It's the vulnerability of those who have the strength to allow themselves to be weak for therein lies their fun and fulfillment.[11]

11 Roly Bain, *Fools Rush In: A Call To Christian Clowning* (London: Marshall Pickerning, 1993), p. 69.

The clown, being of the earth and filled with the breath of God, lives close to the earth. The clown knows of the fallen state of humanity and knows good and evil. This vulnerable lover, totally dependent on a gracious God, lives on the edge of a world turned upside-down by God. Everything the clown does points to glory and praise of God. The clown is free to serve God.

The clown in the circus also has a servant role of filling in between the acts to keep the flow of the circus going smoothly. Unlike the performers, the clown's hard work can be stopped at any moment when the ringmaster blows the whistle. But this least important work gives the most important balance to the circus. I will share much more about the clown as servant in the chapter on Christology.

Again, Dr. Luther expresses, in his explanation to the first article of the Apostles' Creed, how believing in God, the creator of heaven and earth, is lived inside-out through servanthood.

What does this mean?

Answer: I believe that God has created me and all that exists; that he has given me and still sustains my body and soul, all my limbs and senses, my reason and all the faculties of my mind, together with food and clothing, house and home, family and property; that he provides me daily and abundantly with all the necessities of life, protects me from all danger, and preserves me from all evil. All this he does out of his pure, fatherly, and divine goodness and mercy, without any merit or worthiness on my part. For all of this I am bound to thank, praise, serve and obey him. This is most certainly true.[12]

To thank, praise, serve, and obey are the responses of one who is of the earth and lives close to the earth. This least important servant plays the most important role of touching people

12 Book of Concord, p. 345. Again, from Luther's Small Catechism of 1529.

with the heart of the gospel and enabling them to laugh. For the word *humor* and *human* come from the same root word. What is humorous is what is of the earth.[13]

I could not summarize this better than expressed by Rich Bimler in his book, *Angels Can Fly Because They Take Themselves Lightly*:

> Being human is being humorous. It involves not taking yourself so seriously. It is knowing that we will goof things up, and knowing that the Lord still loves and forgives, and gives us another chance. This condition of ours (called sin) continues to focus us back to the cross and the empty tomb for our strength, our purpose, our joy![14]

13 Floyd Shaffer, *If I Were a Clown* (Minneapolis: Augsburg Publishing, 1984), p. 19.

14 Richard Bimler, *Angels Can Fly Because They Take Themselves Lightly* (St. Louis, Mo.: Concordia Publishing House, 1992), p. 25.

Laughter as a Gift from God

When I was a young boy, my parents gave me instructions about behavior in a church building and particularly during a worship service. "Remember, Dick, this is the house of God. This is a holy place," stated my mother, who was helping me to understand the concept of awe.

"There are two things to remember," exclaimed my father. "First, you don't turn around in church. And second, you don't laugh in church." Apparently knowing who is in church and laughing in church went together. My parents were excellent teachers of the faith, but there were some things about the nature of God and the relationship with the people of God that I think they did not know. I never did understand that instruction about not turning around in a worship service and not laughing. How could I not laugh in a worship service? Look who comes! Perhaps that is the connection—if we turn around and look and people look at us, we will laugh. Again, how could we not laugh? God chooses to use ordinary people like you and me, who trip, fall, and stumble in a struggle with sin. God loves us, redeems us, forgives us, and calls us as saints into ministry. That's a laugh! But it seems that many other parents also instructed their children not to turn around and not to laugh in worship because I certainly have not seen much laughter in most worship services.

I have never understood those instructions because from the time I was a child I have pictured God with a smile. I always imagined Jesus laughing with me and laughing with his friends. Before I did the scholastic research I knew that *humor* and *human* came from the same root word. What was humorous to me was what was happening to me and around me. How then could worship not be humorous? Look at who comes. My family laughed all the time at home. I was puzzled. Why wouldn't a gathering of the family of God also be a place of laughter?

Laughter is a sign of an individual's well-being. It is a sign of wholeness in the relationships between individuals. It is a gift from God. I was told that Victor Borge once said, "Laughter is the shortest distance between people." Then, of all places where there should be laughter, it is the church. We are people who share life right next to God and right next to each other because of Christ. We are called to live closely with each other as brothers and sisters in Christ. How could there not be laughter in the worship life of the family of God?

The Hebrew word for "righteous" used often in the Old Testament is *tsaddig*, meaning to walk in a right relationship with God. The covenant-keeping God has taken away the sin and guilt that burden us and prevent us from living close to God.[1] The Greek word for "right-eousness" used in the Septuagint (LXX) for the Hebrew *tsaddig* and in the New Testament, especially by St. Paul, is *dikaiosune*. The meaning is that through the cross of Jesus Christ, God takes

1 Francis Brown, S. R. Driver, and Charles A. Briggs (*A Hebrew and English Lexicon of the Old Testament*, London: Oxford University Press, 1962), pp. 841-843.

away our sin that separates us and brings us back into a right relationship where we live close to God and close to one another.[2] We are restored to a whole relationship with God. If laughter is the shortest distance between people, then it should certainly fill the worship service of the people of God. One cannot live closer than right next to each other in Jesus Christ. God does everything. We can only say "Thank you" as we live in grace and laugh with each other.

John Towsen, in his book *Clowns*, quotes the great clown Otto Griebling:

"If you find yourself able to make people laugh," Otto Griebling believed, "it is a gift of God. You have to do everything from the bottom of our heart. I don't go in for slapstick. I let the emotion come from inside and penetrate the eyes. I'm the same man underneath. I'm always part of the human tragi-comedy."[3]

People who are well can laugh. People who are not well—out of balance with God, others, and self—cannot laugh. They experience dis-ease. Something physical, emotional, or spiritual may have robbed them of their breath. It takes breath to laugh. Some people hold their breath. What then does it mean that there is so little laughter among the family of God and in worship? Could it mean that our relationship with God is not well even though we attend worship?

Or could it be that we believe that laughter may be unholy

2 Gerhard Kittel, translated by Goeffrey W. Bromiley (*Theological Dictionary of the New Testament*, Grand Rapids, Mich.: Wm B. Eerdmans Publishing Co., 1964, Vol. III), pp. 202-210.

3 John H. Towsen, *Clowns* (New York: Hawthorn Books, Inc., 1976), p. 304.

and not connected to God? Is not laughter a gift from God? It is a great question.

In Scripture the words for laughter are used thirty-nine times. In all but one of those times, the meaning of laughter is "to scorn" (2 Kings 19:21; Job 5:22; Psalms 2:4, for a few examples). In these texts laughter is a sign of superiority over one's enemies.

The only exception is the account of Sarah and Abraham in the birth of their son, Isaac. In this exceptional story laughter is a sign of righteous joy. Notice the connection of the two words: *laughter* and *righteous*.

The Jewish Rabbis seldom speak of laughter, even though in many of their writings one finds wonderfully humorous stories. The Hebrews did not ascribe laughter to God. In fact, laughter was the opposite of wisdom. But to the Greeks, laughter was a divine characteristic and inseparable from theophany, visual manifestations of God.[4]

Even though the Hebrew people did not ascribe laughter as an attribute of God, the Creator God was telling Israel and all nations through the Scripture that laughter is a gift from the God of creation. It is difficult for a person to look at the creation accounts in Scripture and not think of laughter and playfulness as gifts of the creator.

In Genesis 1 God speaks a creative word and the chaos of the primal deep and waters were given boundaries and splashed with creative splendor. The chaos explodes into all the colors of creation: trees, flowers, plants, birds, fish, mountains, plains, animals, sky, rivers, seas, sun, moon, stars—the universe! And with each step of creation Creator God responded, "It is good. It is perfect!" (Genesis 1:4, 10, 12, 18, 21, 25, and 31). It is hard to imagine that picture without God smiling and laughing with delight.

The psalmist paints the similar response in Psalm 8 and describes our response to seeing creation and thinking of God. If I were looking at all of creation, I would smile, be filled with joy, delight, and awe. My psalm would be, "Wow!" I probably could

4 Gerhard Kittel, ed., *Theological Dictionary of the New Testament*, Vol. I, pp. 658-660.

say more, but I think that's enough for me! The wonder and delight are a gift from God.

> When I look at your heavens, the work of your fingers, the moon and the stars that you have established; what are human beings that you are mindful of them, mortals that you care for them? *(Psalm 8:3-4)*

I have seen other people laugh and smile as they express the joys, delights, and wonders of creation. At a zoo or in natural habitat, how can one not laugh with delight at otters, a long-necked and -legged giraffe, a duck-billed platypus, a hippopotamus, or a family of primates. These are gifts from God, a God who enjoys laughter and playfulness. For God created the great sea monster, Leviathan, just for fun.

> O Lord, how manifold are your works! In wisdom you have made them all; the earth is full of your creatures. Yonder is the sea, great and wide, creeping things innumerable are there, living things both small and great. There go the ships, and Leviathan that you formed to sport in it. *(Psalm 104: 24-26)*

In Psalm 126 laughter is connected with joy even though the context implies holding something over one's enemies.

> When the Lord restored the fortunes of Zion, we were like those who dream. Then our mouth was filled with laughter, and our tongue with shouts of joy. *(Psalm 126:1-2)*

Laughter connects a person to creation. It comes from deep inside a human being. It is living life inside-out. The Creator shaped humanity out of clay and deep inside put in *ruach*, the breath of God. This breath of God goes in and out, physically and spiritually, and frees a person to laugh. There is healing. Laughter is a gift of God.

The laughter of God prompts the funniest, lovingest,
gentlest, action when God honors a chunk of soil—a
clod from earth—and bestows to it and through it the
gift of life…Maybe "clods" do have a special place in
the wide sweep of creation.[5]

But in the exceptional laughing story of Sarah and Abraham
and the birth of their son, Isaac, is the affirmation that God gives
the gift of laughter as a sign of the wellness of our relationships.
Far too often the faith teachers in our Sunday schools and vacation church schools passed over this story too lightly. Perhaps
they were so serious and intent on the children knowing the
details of the story that they missed the point and didn't laugh.

In Genesis 15 Abram (his name is changed to Abraham later
in Genesis 17) is concerned about God as a promise-keeper.
Abram has done what God had asked him to do and even though
God helped him rescue his nephew, Lot, he was concerned about
other things of God's promise. Abram had cattle, sheep, goats,
gold, silver, servants, tents, a beautiful wife, but he did not have
any children. Abram and Sarai (her name is changed to Sarah
later in Genesis 17) are getting older, beyond the age of having
children. Abram is concerned. How is God going to keep the
promise?

He brought him outside and said, "Look toward heaven
and count the stars, if you are able to count them." Then
he said to him, "So shall your descendants be."
(Genesis 15:5)

Genesis 16 tells the story of folly when the creation tries to
help the Creator keep a promise. When Abram was about 85
years of age and Sarai 75, Sarai came up with a plan. She knew
of her husband's concern. There was a custom at that time that if
a wife was not able to give birth to a child, that the wife could

5 Floyd Shaffer, *If I Were A Clown* (Minneapolis: Augsburg Publishing, 1984), pp.
15 & 16.

give her handmaiden to her husband. He would have sexual inter-course with her, and if she conceived and gave birth to a child, the child would belong to the wife and husband.

I love this story because it is so humorous. Since I am a male, I think of it from the point of Abraham in a culture of extreme male chauvinism. His wife brings in a beautiful young woman and shares the plan for him to have sexual intercourse with her. I can't imagine Abram taking long to make up his mind. In fact, it is the very next verse:

And Abram listened to the voice of Sarai. *(Genesis 16: 2)*

Abram probably didn't listen to all of Sarai's plans, but to this one he listened! Sarai's handmaiden, Hagar, did conceive, and when Abram was 86, Hagar gave birth to a son, Ishmael. But Hagar did not give up her son to Sarai, and despite all the work done by Sarai and Abram to help God keep God's promise, the plan did not work. It was another reminder of the difference between the Creator and creation.

In Genesis 17 the Lord God Almighty appears to Abram. Now Abram is 99 years old. He probably couldn't even spell sex, let alone have it and enjoy it. But the Creator God tells Abram that he will have a son from his wife Sarai and that God will keep the promise. It is here that God changes Abram's name to Abraham and Sarai's name to Sarah. That was more than old Abraham could take. He fell to the ground and burst into laughter.

Then Abraham fell on his face and laughed, and said to himself, "Can a child be born to a man who is a hun-dred years old? Can Sarah, who is ninety years old, bear a child?" And Abraham said to God, "O that Ishmael might live in your sight!" God said, "No, but your wife Sarah shall bear you a son, and you shall name him Isaac." *(Genesis 17:17-19)*

It is God who gives Abraham and Sarah the child. It is God's gift. It is not because of Abraham's virility or a drug like Viagra.

This child is a gift of the God of grace and the God of surprise. Notice that it is God who changes the names of the parents and names the child. He names the child, Isaac, which means, he laughs.[6]

This is an extraordinary story of a man who laughed with God. In fact, he laughed so hard that he fell on his face on the ground. What a relationship Abraham must have had with God. For when I remember times that I laughed so hard that tears welled up inside my eyes and I lost control and fell out of my chair to the floor or to the ground, I remember that I was never alone. Just remembering the time laughing connects me to the friend or friends who were with me. Later, when I attempted to tell others why we laughed so hard, often they don't laugh. So I respond, "I guess you have to be there." It really isn't "being there." It is being in that relationship. It is being in a right relationship. Laughter is a sign of the intimacy of a relationship. It is a time when one is very vulnerable and perhaps most open to the power of God.

It is no wonder that the author of the New Testament letter to the Hebrews used Abraham as a model for living by faith:

> Now faith is the assurance of things hoped for, the conviction of things not seen. Indeed, by faith our ancestors received approval. By faith we understand that the worlds were prepared by the word of God, so that what is seen was made from things that are not visible.... By faith Abraham obeyed when he was called to set out for a place that he was to receive as an inheritance; and he set out, not knowing where he was going. By faith he stayed for a time in the land he had been promised, as in a foreign land, living in tents, as did Isaac and Jacob, who were heirs with him of the same promise. For he looked forward to the city that has foundations, whose

6 Francis Brown, S. R. Driver, and Charles A. Briggs, (*A Hebrew and English Lexicon of the Old Testament*, London: Oxford University Press, 1962), p. 850.

architect and builder is God. By faith he received power of procreation, even though he was too old—and Sarah herself was barren—because he considered him faithful who had promised. Therefore from one person, and this one as good as dead, descendants were born, "as many as the stars of heaven and as the innumerable grains of sand by the seashore." *(Hebrews 11:1-3, 8-12)*

C. Welton Gaddy in his book *God's Clowns* states that laughter is a dynamic dimension of personal faith:

Laughing can be a liberating experience. Persons able to laugh heartily are capable of throwing off those things that bind them unnecessarily and prevent an authentic life. In such laughter and liberty, faith becomes a possibility. Noted theologian Reinhold Niebuhr wisely speaks of humor as a "prelude to faith" and calls laughter "the beginning of prayer."[7]

It is not by accident that the man who laughed with God is one of the great people of faith in the book of Hebrews. Ah, but the story of Abraham and Sarah continues and there is more laughter. Apparently Abraham failed to tell his wife, Sarah, of the laughing time he had with God. Perhaps he thought she wouldn't understand the humor because she wasn't there.

In Genesis 18 the Lord visited Abraham again to remind him of what God has promised. This time, as God was telling the promise of them giving birth to a son, Sarah overhears it from inside the tent near the entrance and Sarah begins to laugh. She knew that she was 89 years of age, but she also knew that Abraham was 99 years old.

So Sarah laughed to herself, saying, "After I have grown old, and my husband is old, shall I have pleasure?" The

7 C. Welton Gaddy. *God's Clowns* (San Francisco: Harper & Row Publishers, 1990), pp. 70-71.

Lord said to Abraham, "Why did Sarah laugh, and say,
'Shall I indeed bear a child, now that I am old?' Is anything too wonderful for the Lord? At the set time I will
return to you, in due season, and Sarah shall have a
son." But Sarah denied, saying, "I did not laugh"; for
she was afraid. He said, "Oh yes, you did laugh."
(Genesis 18:12-15)

Abraham laughed. Sarah laughed. But God had the last
laugh. And because of the surprise of this God of grace the people who live close to this God, in a right relationship, a faithful
relationship, continue to laugh.

Now Sarah said, "God has brought laughter for me;
everyone who hears will laugh with me." And she said,
"Who would ever have said to Abraham that Sarah
would nurse children? Yet I have borne him a son in his
old age." *(Genesis 21:6-7)*

The name Isaac, or "he laughs," is used more than 115 times
in the Scriptures.[8] Often the name is linked to the family of the
covenant as a reminder to the people of the covenant relationship
(Genesis 28:13, 35:13, 50:24; Exodus 32:13; Leviticus 26:42;
Numbers 32:11; Deuteronomy 9:5; 1 Kings 18:36; and many
more). God urges us to remember the covenant relationship.
"Remember I am the God of your fathers: Abraham (father of all
nations), Isaac (laughter), and Jacob (the crooked one)." God's
reminder is a powerful statement of amazing grace. God
describes our relationship. "Remember I am the God whose love
reaches out to all nations. I am the God of the laughter of intimate relationships. And I am your God even when you are off the
path with me." Laughter is a gift from God that reminds us of our
intimate relationships.

God's actions with the heroic characters of the period of the

---

8 Robert Young, *Analytical Concordance to the Bible* (New York: Funk & Wagnalls
   Company, 1964), pp. 520-521.

Judges of Israel provide laugh after laugh. The surprise in Judges 4 and 5 is that God raised up a woman to be Judge. It is under the leadership of Deborah that Israel reached its highest level during this period. Read in Judges 7 how God continued to cut down the number of soldiers for Gideon's battle with the Midianites and God told them not to use any weapons. God did this so that the Israelites would know for certain that Israel did not defeat the Midianites, but God did.

Constantly in the period of the Judges, God used the weak and the outcast to show divine strength and presence. In Judges 11 Jephthah was a family castaway and God raised him to be judge of all of Israel. In Judges 14-16 Samson provided lots of laughs when he constantly teased the Philistines.

Next the period of the great kings of Israel provide more laughs. In 1 Samuel 10:17-27 as the prophet Samuel was introducing the new king, King Saul, son of Kish from the tribe of Benjamin, all of Israel waited to see the chosen king. Think of Samuel as the ringmaster introducing the greatest king of all times: "Ladies and Gentlemen of Israel, Children of Yahweh! I draw your attention to the center ring where I proudly present your new king—Saul, son of Kish!" But Saul doesn't come out. In fact, he is hiding with the baggage. Samuel continues, "Ah…like I said, here he is now, King Saul! Somebody get him out here." What a humorous picture of a coronation this is!

David, the shepherd boy, brings more laughter as he puts on King Saul's armor, size XXXL. David disappears in the armor and it is so heavy that he cannot walk (1 Samuel 17). Even the Philistine, Goliath of Gath, must have laughed when he saw a small boy with no armor come out to fight the giant. Or how about King David's new set of clothes as he danced in the streets of Jerusalem in celebration of the return of the Ark of the Covenant. I am certain David brought more than a chuckle to Judah that day (2 Samuel 6).

The prophets of the Old Testament, much like clowns, perform exaggerated routines, so the people of Judah and Israel will remember the covenant relationship they have with God. But Judah and Israel rarely remember and they do not laugh with God.

One could ask, "Is there any laughter in the life of Jesus?" Although there is no scripture passage stating that Jesus laughed, his relationship with his disciples and his stories are filled with humor. In John 11:35 we read that Jesus wept over the death of his close friend Lazarus. Laughter is the sign of a close relationship. Jesus and Lazarus must have laughed together, especially after Jesus raised him from the dead. Elton Trueblood was one of the first people to write a book on the humor of Jesus.[9] Although Trueblood's book is not very exegetical or systematic, it does give people new insights into the character of Jesus. Trueblood's book helped other people wonder whether or not Jesus laughed. Father Henri Cormier, a member of the Congregation of Jesus and Mary is very convincing that Jesus laughed and used humor in his teachings and relationship with his disciples. In his book, *The Humor of Jesus*, Cormier says:

> We shall discover the following points:
>
> 1. Jesus had a sense of humor.
> 2. Jesus frequently makes use of irony.
> 3. Jesus does not use mockery.
> 4. Probably Jesus laughed.
> 5. "Double meaning" is a key to Jesus' humor.
> 6. The secret of Jesus' humor is his sense of the absolute and of the relative.[10]

It is difficult to think of Jesus' relationship with his disciples without laughter. They rarely understood what Jesus was talking about. Jesus' disciples were a strange mixture of personality types. Perhaps one of the reasons that Jesus selected them was for the laughter they must have provided. There is humor in the relationship with Jesus and the disciples written in Mark 9. They did

---

9 Elton Trueblood, *The Humor of Christ* (New York: Harper & Row, 1964).
10 Henri Cormier, *The Humor of Jesus* (New York: Alba House, 1977), pp. 3,4.

not understand what Jesus was talking about, so they had their
own discussion about their concerns. Then Jesus uses the foolishness of their discussion to make a powerful statement about
power in the kingdom of God. From what follows I doubt the disciples understood this teaching of Jesus either:

> But they did not understand what he [Jesus] was saying
> and were afraid to ask him. Then they came to
> Capernaum; and when he was in the house he asked
> them, "What were you arguing about on the way?" But
> they were silent, for on the way they had argued with
> one another who was the greatest. He sat down, called
> the twelve, and said to them, "Whoever wants to be
> first must be last of all and servant of all." Then he took
> a little child and put it among them; and taking it in his
> arms, he said to them, "Whoever welcomes one such
> child in my name welcomes me, and whoever welcomes
> me welcomes not me but the one who sent me."
> (Mark 9:32-37)

Jesus and his disciples were always eating and drinking with
the society outcasts. According to the Scriptures they attended a
lot of parties. It is hard to imagine that they did not laugh often
with their hosts and with each other. They went to so many parties that they were accused of being gluttons and drunkards:

> The Son of Man came eating and drinking, and they say,
> "Look, a glutton and a drunkard, a friend of tax collec-
> tors and sinners!" Yet wisdom is vindicated by her
> deeds." (Matthew 11:19)

The pictures that Jesus paints in his teaching illustrations
cause one to laugh:

> Again I tell you, it is easier for a camel to go through the
> eye of a needle than for someone who is rich to enter the
> kingdom of God. (Matthew 19:24)

Laughter certainly comes when one imagines of a camel trying to squeeze through the eye of a needle or a very small door
as some scholars say. But I think there is even more laughter in
picturing the disciples trying to figure out what Jesus is telling
them!

When a person sees Jesus smiling and laughing as he taught,
preached, and lived among the people, she has new insights to the
nature of our God. It is a picture of love, laughter, joy, and
delight. Cal Samara thinks it is so important that people see Jesus
smiling and laughing that he has two pages of the names and
addresses of artists who have painted a smiling or laughing
Jesus.[11]

Where then do we look for humor? Like Jesus, we find it
right under our noses. God established it with creation. It is all
over in God's creation from the con-
stellations in the sky to the duck-
billed platypus on the earth. And God
put it in us with the holy breath that
gives life. We see it in the lives of the
judges, the kings, and the prophets.

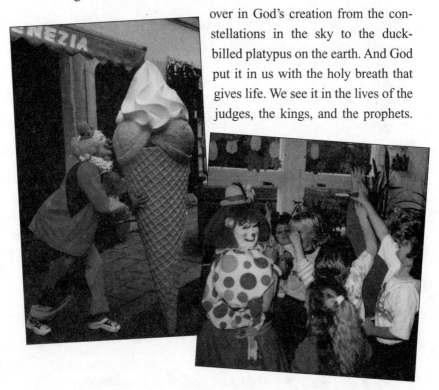

11 Cal Samra, *The Joyful Christ: The Healing Power of Humor* (San Francisco:
Harper & Row Publishers, 1985), pp. 211-212.

Jesus found it in the things of the earth and the people of the earth who surrounded him. He gave new view to the familiar by reframing it with the gospel. Humor and laughter is a way of reframing. It gives a new perspective. That is what Christ clowns do. They create word pictures and reframe them. They are able to do this because they know that God is the giver of laugher. On Easter morning the laughter of God echoed from the empty tomb. Abraham did not have to sacrifice his son, Isaac, for God did sacrifice his son.

From creation to the empty tomb, our God laughs and delights!

Because God does laugh and delight, and because we believe we are created in God's image, we can feel free to let laughter have its place in Christian life. To withhold or suppress laughter in times of joyful praise and worship is not being reverent. It may be Satan's way to confuse us about what a right relationship with God should be. Perhaps a bit more laughter in churches would be a more acceptable sacrifice, one that is sweet to the Almighty.

If I were a clown, I'd laugh with God.[12]

12 Floyd Shaffer, *If I Were a Clown* (Minneapolis: Augsburg Publishing, 1984), p. 20.

Chapter 4 The Foolishness of God

In my 30-plus years as an ordained Lutheran pastor, there has been something about the nature of God that I just do not understand. I understand the God of the law, but I do not understand of the God of the gospel. I understand law and justice. The law describes the relationship, the boundaries of the relationship, the penalty of breaking the relationship, and it guides, accuses, judges, condemns, and holds people accountable. The law makes sense to me. But the good news of a gracious God I do not understand. How can God love and forgive people who do not deserve love, people who forget, and people who sin again and again? A God of grace makes no sense in the culture and world I live in.

To be called to be a pastor or a clown of the gospel can leave a person confused, frustrated, and angry because God doesn't act in a way that makes sense. I understand Jonah's frustration that God did not act toward the people of Nineveh in a manner that made sense to Jonah. Why do all that work, if God is going to act foolishly? I understand why Jonah ran away from God:

> But this was very displeasing to Jonah, and he became angry. He prayed to the Lord and said, "O Lord! Is not this what I said while I was still in my own country? That is why I fled to Tarshish at the beginning; for I knew that you are a gracious God and merciful, slow to anger, and abounding in steadfast love, and ready to relent from punishing." *(Jonah 4:1-2)*

I don't understand how God can change God's mind on very clear issues of sin and consequences. It is grace that I do not understand. It is foolish! I just don't get it! Ah, but the beauty of the gospel is that through faith in Christ I get it even if I don't get it. Now, do you get it?

Grace is filled with foolish talk because the source of grace is a foolish God. God's entire plan from the beginning of creation was foolish.

> Just as he chose us in Christ before the foundation of the world to be holy and blameless before him in love. He destined us for adoption as his children through Jesus Christ, according to the good pleasure of his will, to the praise of his glorious grace that he freely bestowed on us in the Beloved. In him we have redemption through his blood, the forgiveness of our trespasses, according to the riches of his grace that he lavished on us. With all wisdom and insight he has made known to us the mystery of his will, according to his good pleasure that he set forth in Christ, as a plan for the fullness of time, to gather up all things in him, things in heaven and things on earth. *(Ephesians 1:4-10)*

Foolish action is at the heart of this foolish God. The entire gospel message of this foolish God hinges on the resurrection of Jesus, the Christ.

> If Christ has not been raised, your faith is futile and you are still in your sins. Then those also who have died in Christ have perished. If for this life only we have hoped in Christ, we are of all people most to be pitied. *(1 Corinthians 15:17-19)*

> But someone will ask, "How are the dead raised? With what kind of body do they come?" Fool! What you sow does not come to life unless it dies. *(1 Corinthians 15:35)*

St. Paul is in big trouble trying to share the nature of God with the people of Corinth. Corinth was a Greek commercial city. The Greeks prided themselves on being wise. They loved to talk and listen. The Greek philosopher Plato influenced them with his reasoning of the dichotomy of body and soul. The body was evil and the soul as good. When a person died, she was freed from the evil entrapment of the body and the soul would return to the eternal reason (the Greek word is *nous*). So any talk about resurrection of the body was pure foolishness to them.

Paul had run into this same struggle before with the Athenians when he talked to the people standing before the Areopagus. This event is recorded in Acts 17. Paul, noticing that they had statues to every known god and even one to an unknown god, began his talk about this unknown god. He used language of Greek poets. They were all ears listening to Paul talking about the nature of God until he started talking about the resurrection of the dead. Then they walked away from this foolish talk about a foolish God:

> When they heard of the resurrection of the dead, some scoffed; but others said, "We will hear you again about this." (Acts 17:32)

The message of this foolish God does not make sense to Jews or Greeks of the first century. Nor does it make sense to cultures of the 21st century. It leaves clowns, teachers, pastors, and any followers of Jesus very troubled:

> For Jews demand signs and Greeks desire wisdom, but we proclaim Christ crucified, a stumbling block to Jews and foolishness to Gentiles. (1 Corinthians 1:22-23)

The New Testament Greek word for "fool" or "folly" is *mo'rus*, from which we get the English word *moron*. No one wants to be called a moron. St. Paul really struggles with this foolishness of God because he knows that the use of the word *fool* or *folly* in the Old Testament writings of his time do not mean merely "stupid" or "insane." Rather, *folly* is the opposite of *wisdom*, which is always regarded as a gift of revelation. So when Israel disregards divine revelation as in Deuteronomy 32:6, she is declared foolish. The whole book of Proverbs shows wisdom as the opposite of folly. The content of wisdom is detailed in the law. Thus disobedience to the law is folly because it leads to denial of God.[1]

According to the pre-Christian, Greek version of the Old Testament, called the Septuagint, a fool leads astray others who are seeking salvation. For example, in Jeremiah 5:21, what is missing is a true knowledge of God. The people of Judah are not reverent toward Yahweh. They have eyes but do not see and have ears, but do not hear. Thus the folly condemned is apostasy from God.[2]

An interesting use of the Greek word for fool applies to Job in the Septuagint in Job16:7. Becoming a fool is a divine judgment on people who think their wisdom surpasses God's. In Job 16 the Greek word for fool is used along with another word that means "delivered up to decay." The fool is subject to corruption and very vulnerable.[3]

St. Paul is very well aware of this use of the word *fool*. He sees that both he and his churches stand under that burden of being called foolish. Paul recognizes that in the essential judgment of the world, God's actions are foolish and believers are fools. This is the pronouncement of the world, not God's. After the struggle mentioned before with the Greeks at Athens, Paul's struggle with believing in the foolishness of God continued. In Acts 18:15 Gallio considers the dispute between Paul and the Jews as foolish. In Acts 26:24 Festus declares Paul to be out of his mind. Finally, looking through the cross of Jesus Christ, Paul

1 Alan Richardson, *A Theological Word Book of the Bible* (New York: MacMillan Co., 1963), pp. 84, 85.
2 Gerhard Kittel, editor. *Theological Dictionary of the New Testament, Vol. 4* (Grand Rapids, Mich.: Eerdmans, 1967), p. 834.
3 Gerhard Kittel, editor. *Theological Dictionary of the New Testament, Vol. 4*, p. 836.

sees that foolishness is God's miraculous work in the world. God
fixes a value without regard to human assessment:

> For the message about the cross is foolishness to those
> who are perishing, but to us who are being saved it is
> the power of God. For it is written, "I will destroy the
> wisdom of the wise, and the discernment of the discern-
> ing I will thwart." Where is the one who is wise? Where
> is the scribe? Where is the debater of this age? Has not
> God made foolish the wisdom of the world? For since, in
> the wisdom of God, the world did not know God
> through wisdom, God decided, through the foolishness
> of our proclamation, to save those who believe. For Jews
> demand signs and Greeks desire wisdom, but we pro-
> claim Christ crucified, a stumbling block to Jews and
> foolishness to Gentiles, but to those who are called,
> both Jews and Greeks, Christ the power of God and the
> wisdom of God. For God's foolishness is wiser than
> human wisdom, and God's weakness is stronger than
> human strength. Consider your own call, brothers and
> sisters: not many of you were wise by human standards,
> not many were powerful, not many were of noble birth.
> But God chose what is foolish in the world to shame the
> wise; God chose what is weak in the world to shame
> the strong; God chose what is low and despised in the
> world, things that are not, to reduce to nothing things
> that are, so that no one might boast in the presence of
> God. He is the source of your life in Christ Jesus, who
> became for us wisdom from God, and righteousness and
> sanctification and redemption, in order that, as was
> written, "Let the one who boasts, boast in the Lord."
> (1 Corinthians 1:18-31)

Faith seeking understanding through the cross of Christ gives
a person a different vision. Paul perceives that the world claims
that God's actions are foolish and those who proclaim Jesus as the

Messiah are foolish. Those people who believe that the life, death, resurrection, and ascension of Jesus Christ redeem them and reconcile them to God are fools. Paul concludes that if the world sees God and those who believe in the death and resurrection of Christ for our atonement as fools, then we all should become fools for Christ. The whole message is about a gracious God.

This struggle with a faith centered on the foolishness of God is not just a struggle for first-century disciples, followers of Jesus. It is for all centuries. Theologian and New Testament scholar, Dr. Martin Franzmann, described one aspect of being a theologian as knowing one is a fool in a wonderfully written article, "The Marks of the Theologian":

> For the theologian is by Biblical definition a fool, a child, and a slave; they are not impressive entities. A theologian is a fool; it is imperative that he be one: "Let no man deceive himself," St. Paul says: "If any man among you seemeth to be wise in this world, let him become a fool that he may be wise" (1 Corinthians 3:18). We like to deceive ourselves well enough and to think that we have a choice between being fools and something else after all.[4]

> But the theologian is not primarily a scholar, he does not set himself an ideal of scholarship; he becomes a scholar almost accidentally, by being a wholehearted theologian. And he is never in any sense a philosopher. He is a fool, and proud of it. Our prayer as theologians must always be:
>> Accept me, Lord, into Thy school,
>> And graduate me as Thy fool.[5]

But the clown, being of the earth, filled with the life-giving

4 Martin Franzmann, "The Marks of a Theologian," *Concordia Theological Monthly* (St. Louis, Mo.: Concordia Seminary Press) Vol. XXIV (February 1953), p. 81.

5 Martin Franzmann, "The Marks of a Theologian," p. 86.

breath of the Creator God, and living close to the earth, knows the difference between the creator and the creation. The clown knows the right relationship with God is not about understanding, but rather about believing. In the Gospel accounts of the foolish action of God in Jesus Christ, Jesus never asks, "Does this make sense?" But rather Jesus asks, "Do you believe this? Do you love me?"

> Jesus said to her [Martha] "I am the resurrection and the life. Those who believe in me, even though they die, will live, and everyone who lives and believes in me will never die. Do you believe this?" (John 11:25-26)

> When they had finished breakfast, Jesus said to Simon Peter, "Simon son of John, do you love me more than these?" He said to him, "Yes, Lord; you know that I love you." Jesus said to him, "Feed my lambs." A second time he said to him, "Simon son of John, do you love me?" He said to him, "Yes, Lord; you know that I love you." Jesus said to him, "Tend my sheep." He said to him the third time, "Simon son of John, do you love me?" *(John 21:15-17)*

> Now Jesus did many other signs in the presence of his disciples, which are not written in this book. But these are written so that you may come to believe that Jesus is the Messiah, the Son of God, and that through believing you may have life in his name. *(John 20:30-31)*

Faith is about believing, even when one does not see or understand. Understanding does not seek faith. Faith always seeks understanding. The clown is totally immersed, baptized, into the foolishness of Christ. The clown always looks at life and theology through the cross of Christ:

> Now faith is the assurance of things hoped for, the conviction of things not seen. Indeed, by faith our ancestors

received approval. By faith we understand that the worlds were prepared by the word of God, so that what is seen was made from things that are not visible. *(Hebrews 11:1-3)*

So believers in Christ must continue to live as fools and continue to proclaim the foolishness of God. The following is more foolish talk:

Once there was a man who tried to understand the Resurrection. Once when a truck was pouring a sidewalk, he planted a seed in wet cement at night. When the foundation was laid and the building was finished, he went to work there. It was dedicated in the spring when the apple blossoms were out. He looks at the sidewalk every morning.[6]

6 Herbert Brokering, *I Opener* (St. Louis, Mo.: Concordia Publishing House, 1974), p. 24.

Christology of Clown Ministry

O ne of my deep concerns in clown ministry has been the lack of a strong theology in the actions of so many Christian clowns. I do not judge anyone's faith or hearts. For clown ministry to have a strong theology and proclaim the foolishness of God, it is essential to establish a solid, biblical Christology. Christology is at the center of Christian theology. If we want to learn more about God, we must look closely at Jesus, the Christ.

> Jesus once told a beautiful story about a wise man who built a house upon a rock foundation while a foolish man built a house on sand. This story applies to clown ministry.

> A "sandy" foundation of clown ministry is built only upon learning makeup techniques, doing a few religious skits and entertaining at the church social. A "rock" foundation must be built solidly upon Jesus Christ.[1]

C. F. D. Moule, in his book *The Origins of Christology*, argues that the Christology of the New Testament is better under-stood as developmental rather than evolutionary.[2] Thus, in using the symbol of a clown to look closely at Jesus, we should not

1 Floyd Shaffer and Penne Sewall, *Clown Ministry* (Loveland, Colo.: Group Books, 1984), pp. 13,14.

2 C. F. D. Moule, *The Origin of Christology* (Cambridge, England: University Press, 1977), pp. 1-10.

expect to see anything new about God, anything that wasn't there from the beginning. The newness is in the beholder, not in Jesus. The symbol of a clown aids our understanding of Moule's concept of development. It is a growth process from immaturity of faith to maturity of faith. Faith is not in the words of Jesus, but in the very being of Jesus. As we look at Jesus through the symbol of a clown, three major Christological questions are raised:

1. Who is this Jesus?
2. Do I believe this?
3. If Jesus is whom I believe him to be, how will I
   live this faith?

Christology is concerned with the person of Jesus, the Christ, his relation to God on the one hand and to humankind on the other. Most theological books on Christian dogmatics have a large section on Christology. It is because of the unique proclamation by the Christian faith of a God who comes down and becomes a human being and saves a fallen humanity. God acts in and through Jesus Christ. Most writings in Christology focus on the person of Christ as true God and true man; Christ in the state of humiliation and the state of exaltation; and the office of Christ as prophet, priest, and king.

I don't think there is a better tool of theology or symbol to help us know more about God by beholding Jesus Christ than the symbol of a clown and clown ministry. For, as will be explained in great detail later, the clown in ministry literally puts on Christ with makeup, costume, and character. It is why I call a clown in ministry a Christ clown. Imagine yourself with clown makeup and costume on and looking through a huge magnifying glass. We see God most clearly when we look through the cross of Christ. The cross is our magnifying glass. I am hoping in writing this that some clowns will begin to think of how to build props that reflect this key to theology. In Jesus Christ we see God inside-out.

Long ago God spoke to our ancestors in many and various ways by the prophets, but in these last days he has spoken to us by a Son, whom he appointed heir of all things, through whom he also created the worlds. He is the reflection of God's glory and the exact imprint of God's very being, and he sustains all things by his powerful word. *(Hebrews 1:1-3)*

Mark begins his Gospel with a powerful statement about Jesus. Then he takes his reading audience right to the baptism of Jesus. For Mark it is at the baptism of Jesus, the beginning of his ministry, that we begin to see the foolish plan of God unfold. The entire foolish plan centers in Jesus the Christ.

In those days Jesus came from Nazareth of Galilee and was baptized by John in the Jordan. And just as he was coming up out of the water, he saw the heavens torn apart and the Spirit descending like a dove on him. And a voice came from heaven, "You are my Son, the Beloved; with you I am well pleased." *(Mark 1:9-11)*

John the Baptist testifies that his cousin, Jesus, is the promised Messiah. He tells people that if they are looking for the Spirit of God, they should keep their eyes on Jesus. They should behold him from every angle of their lives. John is saying, "Look at Jesus from every angle of your life. This is the one who can change your life." The three questions of Christology keep coming throughout the gospel of John. Use the magnifying glass. What do you see?

The next day he saw Jesus coming toward him and declared, "Here is the Lamb of God who takes away the sin of the world! This is he of whom I said, 'After me comes a man who ranks ahead of me because he was before me.' I myself did not know him; but I came baptizing with water for this reason, that he might be

revealed to Israel." And John testified, "I saw the Spirit
descending from heaven like a dove, and it remained on
him. I myself did not know him, but the one who sent
me to baptize with water said to me, 'He on whom you
see the Spirit descend and remain is the one who bap-
tizes with the Holy Spirit.' And I myself have seen and
have testified that this is the Son of God." *(John 1:29-34)*

Do you see God in Jesus? How would you draw it on paper?
How would you sing it or hum it? How could you tell it without
words? Who else needs to see? How could you help them
behold? Grab the magnifying glass, and let's take another close
look in the Gospel of John.

Philip said to him, "Lord, show us the Father, and we
will be satisfied." Jesus said to him, "Have I been with
you all this time, Philip, and you still do not know me?
Whoever has seen me has seen the Father. How can you
say, 'Show us the Father?' Do you not believe that I am
in the Father and the Father is in me? The words that I
say to you I do not speak on my own; but the Father
who dwells in me does his works." *(John 14:8-10)*

There are no systematically defined and officially author-
ized creeds in the New Testament. Yet, when one looks carefully
into the New Testament, she will see that the church of the New
Testament did sing, pray, preach, exorcise, heal, and testify in the
name of Jesus Christ. In these actions one can see that the content of faith became more or less fixed in creed-like formulas.
For example, Paul states that what he is saying to the church at
Corinth is what he had previously received.

For I handed on to you as of first importance what I in
turn had received: that Christ died for our sins in accordance to the scriptures, and that he was buried, and that
he was raised on the third day in accordance with the

scriptures, and that he appeared to Cephas, then to the twelve. Then he appeared to more than five hundred brothers and sisters at one time, most of whom are still alive, though some have died. Then he appeared to James, then to all the apostles. *(1 Corinthians 15:3-7)*

Christological Confessions are found throughout the New Testament:

He [Jesus] asked them, "But who do you say that I am?" Peter answered him, "You are the Messiah." *(Mark 8:29)*

Therefore I want you to understand that no one speaking by the Spirit of God ever says "Let Jesus be cursed!" and no one can say "Jesus is Lord" except by the Holy Spirit. *(1 Corinthians 12:3)*

Because if you confess with your lips that Jesus is Lord and believe in your heart that God raised him from the dead, you will be saved. *(Romans 10:9)*

Therefore let the entire house of Israel know with certainly that God has made him both Lord and Messiah, this Jesus whom you crucified. *(Acts 2:36)*

The gospel concerning his Son, who was descended from David according to the flesh and was declared to be Son of God with power according to the spirit of holiness by resurrection from the dead, Jesus Christ, our Lord. *(Romans 1:3, 4)*

Without any doubt, the mystery of our religion is great: He was revealed in flesh, vindicated in spirit, seen by angels, proclaimed among Gentiles, believed in throughout the world, taken up in glory. *(1 Timothy 3:16)*

Who, though he was in the form of God, did not regard
equality with God as something to be exploited, but
emptied himself, taking the form of a slave, being born in
human likeness. And being found in human form, he
humbled himself and became obedient to the point of
death—even death on a cross. Therefore God also highly
exalted him and gave him the name that is above every
name, so that at the name of Jesus every knee should
bend, in heaven and on earth and under the earth, and
every tongue should confess that Jesus Christ is Lord, to
the glory of God the Father. *(Philippians 2:6-11)*

To clarify the Christian faith against various heresies like
Ebionism, Monarchianism, Docetism, Gnostism, Arianism, and
many more, the church developed creeds.[3] The three great ecumenical creeds of the Christian church are the Apostles' Creed,
the Nicene Creed, and the Athanasian Creed. Each of these
creeds has a strong Christology even though they were developed
over the centuries to combat various distortions of the Christian
faith. The church continues to develop Christology as people of
different cultures and eras raise the question "Who is this Jesus?"

In my own tradition as an ordained pastor of the Lutheran
Church, there is great attention to the understanding of the
Christology of the Reformation period.

The Reformation ushered in a new era in creed-making.
Protestant insistence upon the supreme authority of the
Bible meant that no creed is infallible or of final authority. One consequence was a creedal multiplicity that had
not existed since the third and fourth centuries. Because
the Reformation involved a dispute within the Christian
community as to the nature of Christian faith, more
comprehensive statements of the faith were demanded
than had hitherto been needed. The Reformation creeds

3 J. N. D. Kelly, *Early Christian Doctrines* (New York: Harper & Row, 1960),
pp. 138-162; 280-342.

emphasize in particular those issues that were especially in conflict, such as the doctrines of grace, faith, justification, the church, and sacraments.[4]

You will see from what follows how the second article to the Apostles' Creed was a summary statement developed by the church through the ages. But the Reformation asked for further definition. So in 1529, in the Small Catechism, Martin Luther wrote a further description answering the question of "Who is Jesus?" to deal with the theological issues of his time.

THE SECOND ARTICLE: REDEMPTION

And in Jesus Christ, his only son, our Lord: who was conceived by the Holy Spirit, born of the virgin Mary, suffered under Pontius Pilate, was crucified, dead, and buried: he descended into hell, the third day he rose from the dead, he ascended into heaven, and is seated on the right hand of God, the Father almighty, whence he shall come to judge the living and the dead?

WHAT DOES THIS MEAN?

ANSWER: I believe that Jesus Christ, true God, begotten of the Father from eternity, and also true man, born of the virgin Mary, is my Lord, who has redeemed me, a lost and condemned creature, delivered me and freed me from all sins, from death, and from the power of the devil, not with silver and gold but with his holy and precious blood and his innocent sufferings and death, in order that I may be his, live under him in his kingdom, and serve him in everlasting righteousness, innocence, and blessedness, even as he is risen from the dead and lives and reigns to all eternity. This is most certainly true.[5]

4 J. H. Leith, editor, *Creeds of the Churches* (Garden City, N.Y.: Anchor Books, Doubleday & Company, 1963), pp. 61, 62.

5 Theodore G. Tappert, editor, The Book of Concord (St. Louis, Mo.: Concordia Publishing House, 1959), p. 345.

The history of the creeds and confessions of the faith are helpful tools of Christology. I am suggesting that looking at Christ as a clown and through the eyes of a clown is also helpful in dealing with the three questions of Christology and the foolishness of God. Some Christians struggle with the clown symbol when it is used to illuminate the nature of Christ because they are forced to look at the message of Scripture as comedy. That causes tension because we do not use the Word in its original dramatic sense. We usually think of comedy as not being serious, and the Bible and the church are certainly serious.

Aristophanes understood the drama of comedy or folly. In his introduction to the works of Aristophanes, Moses Hadas writes:

> In comedy alone do men drop the rigid poses they are given in graver kinds of writing and walk and talk on a level with their fellow citizens. It is incongruity, not sympathy for an impoverished gentleman, that makes us laugh at a top hat that is dented or worn with patched shoes.[6]

The Christology of the New Testament partakes of the drama of comedy as well as tragedy, resurrection, and death. It helps us look at the foolish plan of God in Christ. Knowing who this Jesus is informs us of how clowns are to be in ministry and how Christians are to live. A God who comes down on the same level as creation is certainly incongruous with power and authority. Looking at Jesus and talking about him as a clown is incongruous with many of the historical images proclaimed by the church. For some people, thinking of comedy in the Bible and Jesus as a clown is blasphemy. In 1964, a film entitled *The Parable* was shown in the Protestant pavilion at the World's Fair in New York. In this film the Christ figure is shown as a clown. Seeing Christ as a clown touched some and annoyed others, just as did the characters in the movie itself.

6 Moses Hadas, *The Complete Plays of Aristophanes* (New York: Bantam Books, 1962) p. 2.

Harvey Cox in *The Feast of Fools* devotes an entire chapter, "Christ the Harlequin," to the symbol of the clown as a helpful way to behold the foolishness of God in Christ.

> Furthermore, even in the Biblical portrait of Christ there are elements that easily suggest clown symbols. Like the jester, Christ defies custom and scorns crowned heads. Like a wandering troubadour, he has no place to lay his head. Like the clown in the circus parade, he satirizes existing authority by riding into town replete with regal pageantry when he has no earthly power. Like a minstrel he frequents dinners and parties. At the end he is costumed by his enemies in a mocking caricature of royal paraphernalia. He is crucified amidst sniggers and taunts with a sign over his head that lampoons his laughable claim.[7]

The clown is not only a legitimate symbol for studying Christology but perhaps one of the few symbols that we can literally put on. We can see the foolishness of God in the incarnation.

Jesus, Clod Incarnate

The prologue to the Gospel of John suggests incarnation in a unique way. The effects of the incarnation are that we may know and behold God in a new way.

> In the beginning was the Word, and the Word was with God, and the Word was God. He was in the beginning with God. All things came into being through him, and without him not one thing came into being. What has come into being in him was life, and the life was the light of all people. The light shines in the darkness , and the darkness did not overcome it.

7 Harvey Cox, *The Feast of Fools*, (Cambridge, Mass.: Harvard University Press, 1969), pp. 140-141.

There was a man sent from God, whose name was John.
He came as a witness to testify to the light, so that all
might believe through him. He himself was not the light,
but he came to testify to the light. The true light, which
enlightens everyone, was coming into the world.

He was in the world, and the world came into being
through him; yet the world did not know him. He came
to what was his own, and his own people did not
accept him. But to all who received him, who believed
in his name, he gave power to become children of God,
who were born, not of blood or of the will of the flesh
or the will of man, but of God.

And the Word became flesh and lived among us, and we
have seen his glory, the glory as of a father's only son,
full of grace and truth. (John testified to him and cried
out, "This was he of whom I said, 'He who comes after
me ranks ahead of me because he was before me.'")
From his fullness we have all received, grace upon
grace. The law indeed was given through Moses; grace
and truth came through Jesus Christ. No one has ever
seen God. It is God the only Son, who is close to the
Father's heart, who has made him known. *(John 1:1-18)*

In an article entitled "Christology and Controversy" Robert
Kysar, professor of religion, Hamline University, points out five
unique contributions of the prologue of John to New Testament
Christology.[8] First, the prologue affirms Christ's pre-existence in
an absolute way. The uniqueness of the Greek word (*arché*) for
"beginning" stands out sharply when contrasted with the use of
the word in Colossians 1:15 and 18:

He is the image of the invisible God, the firstborn of all
creation *(v. 15)*; He is the head of the body, the church,

8 Robert Kysar, "Christology and Controversy," *Currents in Theology and Mission*
(St. Louis, Mo.: Christ Seminary/Seminex, December 1978), Vol. 5, No.6, pp.
348-368.

he is the beginning, the firstborn from the dead, so that
he might come to have first place in everything *(v. 18)*.

The author of the prologue to John's Gospel asserts the pre-
existence of Christ in a more radical fashion than other New
Testament writers. John leaves no doubt of the importance of this
Jesus. He was before the beginning and in the beginning. The
prologue pushes the existence of Christ beyond the reaches of
human reason or imagination.[9]

The second unique contribution of the prologue is a pattern
of exaltation even through humiliation. Kysar suggests that the
Christological hymn of the prologue was never intended to be
complete without the remainder of John's Gospel. He wanted the
readers to know how important this Jesus is. Like a side-show
barker or a ringmaster, John uses the prologue to invite the reading audience into the story to see the whole story, the entire circus in his Gospel. "Ladies and Gentlemen, Children of All Ages,
I draw your attention to the center ring of the Holy Trinity. The
greatest show on earth proudly presents the one who was with
God from the beginning and is God—Jesus, the Christ. Watch
him closely as he shows us the foolishness of God!"

The drama filled with comedy and tragedy continues to
unfold. In John 1:14, the Word takes on flesh and becomes a clod,
a true human being in Jesus. God stoops down so that we can see
the Creator God in a new, foolish way. It is in the humanity of
Jesus that we behold the new communication of the nature of
God. The Christ is seen in Jesus' life (ministry), death, resurrection, and ascension.

Like the work of a clown, the message is communicated
more indirectly in the humanity of Jesus. The hymn in John's prologue shows Jesus as a human who lives among other humans,
yet with the majesty and power of the divine. This is the third
unique contribution of the prologue. But the reaction of many is

9 Robert Kysar, *Augsburg Commentary on the New Testament–John* (Minneapolis:
Augsburg Publishing House, 1986), pp. 27-34.

that of resistance to such a foolish message in Jesus, just like the
reaction of some of the characters shown in the movie, *The
Parable*.

It was resistance to the truth and light that confronted people
in the incarnate Word. This resistance is shown in the prologue in
the dichotomies of darkness/light, God/flesh, and true/false.

The fourth unique contribution of the prologue is the polem-
ical tone of the prologue. This Christological hymn reflects a
believing community that was under attack. The community was
forced to look at the question "Who is this Jesus?" in a new way.
Others were saying that too much importance was being put on
Jesus. The prologue, as well as the rest of John's Gospel, clearly
proclaims Jesus is the center of all of the foolishness of God.

The fifth contribution of the prologue is the exegesis of the
very being of God. In his conclusion Robert Kysar affirms C. F. D.
Moule's argument of developmental Christology. Jesus is the
greatest show on earth, and this is a story for children of all ages.

> They viewed Christological reflection as an ongoing
> process by which believers are forced again and again
> to re-evaluate affirmations and again and again refor-
> mulate what it is they wish to say. I suggest that this
> mode of theological reflection is one appropriate not
> alone for the crisis of that of Jewish-Christian, con-
> frontation, but for Christian community of any age, and
> most especially our own.[10]

The message of a God who comes down to earth and
becomes human is so foolish that Professor Maurice Wiles, an
Anglican theologian, at the time of the writing of his book, H.G.
Wood, professor of theology at the University of Birmingham,
England, proposed the question, "Could there be Christianity
without the incarnation?" Incarnation doesn't make any sense.[11]

10 Robert Kysar, "Christology and Controversy," *Currents in Theology and Mission*, p. 364.
11 John Hick, editor, *The Myth of God Incarnate* (Philadelphia: Westminster Press, 1977), pp. 1-10.

The heart of the meaning of Christ, the clown, is wrapped up in the incarnation. Jesus is God's down-to-earth talk to his creation. He is the Word of God made flesh, a clod. The incarnation is part of God's foolish plan for creation to see the loving and gracious nature of God. Without the incarnation we will not see the hiddenness and unity of the God of creation and the God of redemption. Without the incarnation Jesus then becomes merely a religious genius or the perfect man of the Arian heresy. The prologue of the Gospel of John clearly and loudly proclaims that Jesus is true God and true man.

The Danish theologian, Regin Prenter, affirms that Jesus, the clown, the incarnate redeemer, is the center of Christology:

> The incarnation is the event through which God unites his creative purpose with his redemptive purpose. God the Creator becomes a creature himself in order to repair the damage which sin had done to created human life. The intention of the idea of the incarnation is to declare that through the event of the atonement it is none other than the Creator himself who is active in order to complete his creative work.
>
> The atonement is the event through which God carries out his redemptive purpose by an act which appears to be the very opposite of his creative purpose. As Creator, God fights against the powers of destruction, forcing them back. Through redemption, however, God allows himself to be overcome by them, to be judged by the law, to become the object of wrath and the punishment of death. In doing so, however, he conquers the destructive powers and thus completes his creative purpose. The idea of atonement declares that through the event of the incarnation God completes his creative purpose by paradoxically becoming a creature himself and taking upon himself the conditions of a condemned man. The incarnation and the atonement cannot be separated

from one another any more than they can be confused
with one another. The incarnation points to the hidden
unity of the atonement; the atonement points to the
manifest duality of the incarnation.[12]

Jesus, the clod incarnate, gives us a way to see the Creator
God inside-out.

Jesus, Trans-rational Clown

One of the interesting characteristics of clowns is that they know
and exemplify that many things in life do not make sense. What
is illogical may be true. Clowns are not confined to logical
boundaries of space and time. Inanimate objects, events, and
even people can provide new meaning to life even when they are
not logical. Jan Mordenski wrote a wonderful parable, *Gabella,
the One, True Clown*, that Alba House Communications made
into a filmstrip. I have used it often in teaching the theology of
clown ministry. Throughout the story Gabella struggles with
what is true and what is logical. He has a high regard for logic,
but is searching for truth.

"You're true. In fact, you're the one true clown." [said
Ronnie]

"I am not sure I understand." [said Gabella]

"He who is truly happy doesn't always understand. You
are truly happy."

Gabella laughed, "I could have told you that."

"I should have known you are the one true clown. Even
when you are crying, you are happy in a way. Happiness
allows for truth, and truth sooner or later brings happiness." [said Ronnie]

12 Regin Prenter, *Creation and Redemption* (Philadelphia: Fortress Press, 1967),
p. 404.

Gabella smiled, "But is it logical that one is happy when one cries?"

Ronnie answered, "It isn't logical, but it's true."[13]

Jesus, like Gabella, is more concerned with the truth, than with logic.

Jesus said to him, "I am the way, and the truth, and the life. No one comes to the Father except through me. "
(John 14: 6)

[Jesus said] "Very truly , I tell you, the one who believes in me will also do the works that I do and, in fact, will do greater works than these, because I am going to the Father." *(John 14:12)*

"If you love me, you will keep my commandments. And I will ask the Father, and he will give you another Advocate, to be with you forever. This is the Spirit of truth, whom the world cannot receive, because it neither sees him nor knows him. You know him, because he abides with you, and he will be in you." *(John 14:15-17)*

"When the Advocate comes, whom I will send to you from the Father, the Spirit of truth who comes form the Father, he will testify on my behalf." *(John 15:26)*

"I still have many things to say to you, but you cannot bear them now. When the Spirit of truth comes, he will guide you into all the truth; for he will not speak on his own, but will speak whatever he hears, and he will declare to you the things that are to come."
(John 16:12, 13)

"Sanctify them in the truth; your word is truth. As you have sent me into the world, so I have sent them into

13 Jan Mordenski illustrated by Mary Grassell, *Gabella, The One True Clown* (Canfield, Ohio: Alba House Communications, 1979), pp. 48-51.

the world. And for their sakes I sanctify myself, so that
they also may be sanctified in truth." (John 17:17-19)

Throughout the Sermon on the Mount in Matthew 5-9 Jesus
says, "You have heard it said...but I say to you..." (Matthew 5:
21-22, 27-28, 31-32, 33-34, 38-39, 43-44). Jesus goes beyond the
rational understanding of the law. He has not come to abolish the
law, rather Jesus fulfills the law and is trans-rational.

If New Testament Christology asked the question "Does this
make sense?" or "Is this rational?" then we would miss the whole
point of life and the foolishness of God. Trans-rational means
going beyond human understanding.[14] Thus, again looking at the
incarnation, the fact that it is not logical for God to become a
human, does not negate the event. Making sense out of the incarnation seems to be the basis for John Hicks and other writers in
The Myth of God Incarnate. Maurice Wiles, the author of chapter one, proposes to consider Christianity without the incarnation
because it is more reasonable.[15] The clown is well aware that the
incarnation does not make sense. That does not mean the incarnation is irrational, but trans-rational. The cognitive is important.
But truth is more important than logic. Reason does not lead one
to faith. But faith always seeks understanding.

I continue to be amazed at how the question "Does this make
sense?" still seems to be used by both liberals and conservatives
within their Christologies. John Hicks would be considered a lib-
eral theologian and, as was mentioned above, and logic is the
basis of his book. Yet Dr. D. James Kennedy, a very conservative
American theologian, uses this same question in his outline of
presenting the gospel to another person. He created a ministry
called Evangelism Explosion.

Several years ago, while I was taking the on-the-job training
course with Dr. Kennedy, I discovered that he, too, believes that

---

14 *Trans-rational* is a descriptive word for a clown that the Rev. Floyd Shaffer used
in tape #1 of *Clown Ministry Workshop* (Pittsburgh, Pa.: Recycle Faith and
Fantasy, Inc., 1979).

15 John Hicks, editor, *The Myth of God Incarnate* (Philadelphia, The Westminster
Press, 1977), p. 5.

one of the questions of Christology is "Does this make sense to you?" In Evangelism Explosion this question is asked the listener following a gospel outline presentation of who Jesus is.[16] John Hicks and D. J. Kennedy are light years apart theologically and yet both think that logic is the important issue of Christology.

In Peter's declaration about Jesus in the synoptic Gospels, the question asked by Jesus was "But who do you say that I am?" (Matthew 16:13-20; Mark 8:27-30; Luke 9:18-21). Peter's response is, "You are the Christ, the Son of the living God." Jesus shows that reason did not lead Peter to this statement of faith. In fact, in Matthew's Gospel, Jesus shows that Peter's statement of faith is trans-rational. It came from the Father because flesh and blood cannot make sense out of it. Then Jesus proceeds to say that the church will be built on the rock of a trans-rational statement of faith. The church will be built on a rock because it comes from God, not from Peter's reason.

When the disciples ask Jesus, "Who is the greatest in the kingdom of heaven?" Jesus' response goes past the values of reason of that culture by pointing out that a child is the greatest. Again, Jesus the trans-rational clown, shows how important is the child. Truth is of more value than reason.

> He called a child, whom he put among them, and said, "Truly I tell you, unless you change and become like a child, you will never enter the kingdom of heaven. Whoever becomes humble like this child is the greatest in the kingdom of heaven. Whoever welcomes one such child in my name welcomes me."

> "If any of you put a stumbling block before one of these little ones who believe in me, it would be better for you if a great millstone were fastened around your neck and you were drowned in the depth of the sea." *(Matthew 18:2-6; also compare Mark 9: 35-37 and Luke 18:15-17)*

16 D. James Kennedy, *Evangelism Explosion* (Wheaton, Ill.: Tyndale House Publishers, 1977), pp. 41, 67, and 177. Dr. Kennedy is pastor of Coral Ridge Church in Ft. Lauderdale, Florida, and the founder of Evangelism Explosion.

The healing miracles of Jesus in the Gospels show that faith is more than having a few logical answers judged as correct by the community. Jesus healed the daughter of the Canaanite woman in Matthew 15 not because of reason, but because of her faith. This story raises more questions, than gives answer, for faith is seeking understanding.

> Just then a Canaanite woman from that region came out and started shouting, "Have mercy on me, Lord, Son of David; my daughter is tormented by a demon." But he did not answer her at all. And his disciples came and urged him, saying, "Send her away for she keeps shouting after us." He answered, "I was sent only to the lost sheep of the house of Israel." But she came and knelt before him, saying, "Lord, help me." He answered, "It is not fair to take the children's food and throw it to the dogs." She said, "Yes, Lord, yet even the dogs eat the crumbs that fall from their masters' table." Then Jesus answered her, "Woman, great is your faith! Let it be done for you as you wish." And her daughter was healed instantly. (Matthew 15:21-28)

In the healing of the blind man in John 9, neither the blind man nor his parents can make sense out of the event. The Pharisees keep trying to rationalize the whole event and cannot see themselves. They are the ones who are blinded by their reason. When Jesus returns to the man, he doesn't ask, "Does this make sense?" Although the story is of a healing of physical blindness of the man, the central message of this section is on the spiritual blindness of the Jewish leaders.

> Jesus heard that they had driven him out, and when he found him, he said, "Do you believe in the Son of Man?" He answered, " Who is he, sir? Tell me, so that I may believe in him." Jesus said to him, "You have seen him and the one speaking with you is he." He said, "Lord, I believe." (John 9:35-38)

In John 11 at the death of Lazarus the entire event is beyond reason. Lazarus had been dead for four days and the body had already started to decay. Jesus called Lazarus and raised him from the dead. Truth is more important than reason. But some of the Pharisees, after being told the story of Jesus and Lazarus, were spiritually blinded by their reason. It led them to plot against Jesus.

> So the chief priests and the Pharisees called a meeting of the council, and said, "What are we to do? This man is performing many signs. If we let him go on like this, everyone will believe in him, and the Romans will come and destroy both our holy place and our nation." But one of them, Caiaphas, who was high priest that year, said to them. "You know nothing at all! You do not understand that it is better for you to have one man die for the people than to have the whole nation destroyed." *(John 11:47-50)*

Jesus, the trans-rational clown has a high value on truth and faith. He shows that depending on reason can lead a person to spiritual blindness. As Regin Prenter expresses it:

> And the picture of the Redeemer God is seen only through faith in the gospel of the incarnation and atonement. Where this gospel is not proclaimed and believed, the idol reason remains, whether it be in some religious form or a theistic form as a denial of the gods of the religions and the myth.[17]

The clown does not try to control life with reason, rather the clown walks on the high wire of life balanced with one foot in faith and the other in fantasy. The clown has a high regard for logic, but seeks truth over reason. For the clown, faith always seeks understanding. Understanding does not seek faith.

17 Regin Prenter, *Creation and Redemption* (Philadelphia: Fortress Press, 1967), p. 420.

It is so human to try to rationalize God and systematically study God's action so that we have all the answers to life. Is not that the purpose of seminaries and theological schools—to teach us the answers? Does not the knowledge of the answers make one a better pastor or teacher of faith? The answer is "No!" Theological training enables a person to seek understanding through faith. From faith come questions. Jesus, the trans-rational clown, shows us the folly of boxing up faith and theology into neat, logical answers. Jesus' teaching and examples always raise new questions about faith.

Jesus, Vulnerable Clown

Through an aggressive act of beholding in Scripture one sees Jesus as one who displays the greatest attribute of a clown, a vulnerable lover. As Jesus gives love away, he leaves himself wide open for misunderstanding, misuse, and attack. The foolishness of God is truly exposed in Jesus. Jesus has a passion for all people, especially the poor and outcasts living on the fringes of life. Jesus is moved by compassion to help people.

> When he saw the crowds, he had compassion for them, because they were harassed and helpless, like sheep without a shepherd. *(Matthew 9:36)*

> A leper came to him begging him, and kneeling he said to him, "If you choose, you can make me clean." Moved with pity, Jesus stretched out his hand and touched him, and said to him, "I do choose. Be made clean!" *(Mark 1:40-42)*

> When the Lord saw her, he had compassion for her and said to her, "Do not weep." Then he came forward and touched the bier, and the bearers stood still. And he said, "Young man, I say to you rise." The dead man sat up and began to speak, and Jesus gave him to his mother. *(Luke 7:13-15)*

(Also see Matthew 14:14, 15:32, 18:27, 20:34; Mark 6:34, 8:2, 9:22; Luke 10:33, 15:20)

In Jesus we see the innards, the heart of God. Jesus heals the sick, feeds the crowds, forgives sins, raises the dead, and casts out demons. Jesus takes the risk of caring for those the community has declared hopeless. Jesus takes risks as he exposes the nature of God.

The New Testament Greek word translated as "moved by compassion" is *splanknizomai*, which originally denoted the inward parts of a sacrifice and can mean the sacrifice itself.[18] Jesus exposes the love of God. He is vulnerable all the way to the cross. In the Gospels' passion narratives, Jesus is before Herod and never speaks a word (Luke 23:6-11). Isaiah described it:

> All we like sheep have gone astray; we have all turned to our own way, and the Lord has laid on him the iniquity of us all. He was oppressed, and he was afflicted, yet he did not open his mouth; like a lamb that is led to the slaughter and like a sheep that before its shearers is silent, so he did not open his mouth. *(Isaiah 53:6-7)*

Jesus was misunderstood by the crowds, the Pharisees, Scribes, and even his own disciples often missed the point. When Jesus talked about his journey to the cross, his disciples want him to talk about something else. But the actions of Jesus caused people to continue to ask, "Who is this Jesus?" Not only in the life of Jesus is the foolishness of God exposed, but love and righteousness come together in the death of Jesus. In the death of Jesus, God lays open his love:

> For while we were still weak, at the right time Christ died for the ungodly. Indeed, rarely will anyone die for a righteous person—though perhaps for a good person

---

18 Gerhard Kittel, editor, *Theological Dictionary of the New Testament* (Grand Rapids, Mich.: Eerdmans, 1967),Vol. 7, pp. 548-559.

someone might actually dare to die. But God proves his
love for us in that while we still were sinners Christ died
for us. Much more surely then, now that we have been
justified by his blood, will we be saved through him
from the wrath of God. For if while we were enemies,
we were reconciled to God through the death of his
Son, much more surely, having been reconciled, will we
be saved by his life. *(Romans 5:6-10)*

Again in the Letter to the Romans, Paul shows that righteousness and love come together in the sacrifice of Jesus, the
vulnerable lover:

He who did not withhold his own Son, but gave him up
for all of us, will he not with him also give us everything
else? *(Romans 8:32)*

In the conclusion of the Nicodemus story, John shows the
foolishness of God's plan and exposes divine love in Jesus' death:

And just as Moses lifted up the serpent in the wilder-
ness, so must the Son of Man be lifted up, that whoever
believes in him may have eternal life. For God so loved
the world that he gave his only Son, so that everyone
who believes in him may not perish but may have eternal life. *(John 3:14-16)*

Also in the epistles of John the love of God is exposed for us
through the vulnerable lover, Jesus:

God's love was revealed among us in this way: God sent
his only Son into the world so that we might live
through him. In this is love, not that we loved God but
that he loved us and sent his Son to be the atoning sacrifice for our sins. *(1 John 4:9-10)*

Notice that in this epistle of John (also in 1 John 2:2) John not only refers to the death of Christ, but he also speaks of the risen Lord and of the full work of Jesus—his incarnation, life, death, and resurrection. Prenter states that through the vulnerable lover, Jesus, the hidden mercy of God is revealed:

> Only in the picture of the righteous love, which reveals itself through incarnation and atonement, do we clearly see the picture of the holy mercy, which reveals itself in creation.[19]

Jesus, the Mediator Clown

Clowns make connections. They connect what is with what could be. They connect inanimate objects with animate characteristics. They connect the generations with joy and laughter. They connect the extremes of life. Like bridges, they bring people to different points. Like reconcilers they bring different points to people. Clowns live the point, act out the point, exaggerate the point, and share the point. Clowns are mediators.

Jesus, the mediator clown, makes connections. Jesus connects the hidden love of God in creation with the love shown in the atonement. Jesus is an intercessor, reconciler, peacemaker, propitiator, and mediator between God and a fallen creation. Like the clown in the circus, Jesus connects faith and fantasy, humanity and deity, law and gospel, sin and grace, death and resurrection, earth and heaven. Like a clown, Jesus connects life with bridges of promise and hope:

> With all wisdom and insight he has made known to us the mystery of his will, according to his good pleasure that he set forth in Christ, as a plan for the fullness of time, to gather up all things in him, things in heaven and things on earth. *(Ephesians 1:9,10)*

19 Regin Prenter, *Creation and Redemption* (Philadelphia: Fortress Press, 1967), p. 420.

Through Jesus, the Christ, God acts out the foolish plan of connecting all people with the truth of salvation. Jesus is the mediator of God's second covenant:

This is right and is acceptable in the sight of God our Savior, who desires everyone to be saved and to come to the knowledge of the truth. For there is one God; there is also one mediator between God and human- kind, Christ Jesus, himself human, who gave himself a ransom for all. *(1 Timothy 2:3-5)*

But Jesus has now obtained a more excellent ministry, and to that degree he is the mediator of a better covenant, which has been enacted through better prom- ises. *(Hebrews 8:6)*

For this reason he is the mediator of a new covenant, so that those who are called may receive the promised eternal inheritance, because a death has occurred that redeems them from the transgressions under the first covenant. *(Hebrews 9:15)*

Jesus, the mediator, brings people into the presence of almighty God without fear and trembling. His sacrifice on the cross paid the penalty for our sins so that we could stand with the righteous before almighty God:

But you have come to Mount Zion and to the city of the living God, the heavenly Jerusalem and to innumerable angels in festal gathering, and to the assembly of the firstborn who are enrolled in heaven, and to God the judge of all, and to the spirits of the righteous made perfect, and to Jesus, the mediator of a new covenant, and to the sprinkled blood that speaks a better word than the blood of Abel. *(Hebrews 12:22-24)*

Do you see the picture? It's a clown routine. Sin, Grace, Fear, Joy, Sad, and Happy are all clowns out of balance. They walk in chaos. In the midst of this chaos comes the mediator clown, Christ. Jesus puts big hands on the ends of the cross. Through the cross Jesus, the mediator clown, connects Sin and Grace, Fear and Joy, Sad and Happy. They hug each other and circle the cross. Connected to each other by the love from the cross, they stand before the holy presence of God as people of the new covenant.

Jesus, the mediator clown, surprises people with his connections. Some people brought a paralytic to Jesus (Mark 2:1-12). They said, "Heal!" But Jesus said, "Forgiven!" Some didn't get the connection so they said, "Blasphemy!" They still didn't get the connection so Jesus said, "Walk." Still some said, "Huh?" They didn't get the connection of Jesus and God, forgiveness and wellness. But the paralytic got the connection. For he walked.

And the people, like those who have seen Ringling Bros. and Barnum & Bailey Circus for the first time, say, "We have never seen anything like this!" Jesus, the mediator clown, makes connections that help people see things about God for the first time. It leads them to ask a question of Christology, "Who is this Jesus?"

In Luke 7:36-50, Jesus, the mediator clown, surprises the Pharisee by connecting a sinful woman with forgiveness and the ministry of hospitality and with faith. The Pharisee prided himself on doing right things and keeping all 613 laws perfectly. But he forgot about the very important ministry of hospitality. The sinful woman used everything she had to welcome Jesus. Jesus connects the greatness of her sin with the even greater gift of forgiveness and her response to God's grace was her great love. Jesus connects the Pharisee's lack of gratefulness with his lack of love and hospitality. Jesus connects the brokenness of the sinful woman's with peace. And the others at the table ask a question of Christology, "Who is this who even forgives sins?"

Jesus, like the advance clown of the circus, prepares the city of Jerusalem for the greatest show on earth. In Matthew 21 we see how Jesus connects God and the fallen creation. Jesus, the mediator clown, rides through the city on a donkey. Some people get the connection. They spread their cloaks on the road, cut branches, waved palm branches, and shouted, "Hosanna to the Son of David! Blessed is the one who comes in the name of the Lord! Hosanna in the highest heaven!" Again, the action of Jesus and the response of those who got the connection raised others to ask, "Who is this?" But later in the week, when Jesus was on trial, crucified, and died, very few got the connection.

In Luke 22 Jesus connects old covenant with new covenant, the Passover with the Eucharist. Jesus, the mediator clown, tells of God's foolish decision of the way of the cross. In the Eucharist, Jesus again connects fallen sinners with forgiveness and grace. Jesus, the mediator clown, connects the forgiven people to God and to one another. Remember?

> When the hour came, he took his place at the table, and the apostles with him. He said to them, "I have eagerly desired to eat this Passover with you before I suffer; for I tell you, I will not eat it until it is fulfilled in the kingdom of God." Then he took a cup, and after giving thanks he said, "Take this and divide it among yourselves; for I tell you that form now on I will not drink of the fruit of the vine until the kingdom of God comes." Then he took a loaf of bread, and when he had given thanks, he broke it and gave it to them, saying, "This is my body, which is given for you. Do this in remembrance of me." And he did the same with the cup after supper, saying, "This cup that is poured out for you is the new covenant in my blood." *(Luke 22:14-21)*

Jesus, again, is the mediator between God the Father and fallen humanity:

> Everyone therefore who acknowledges me before others, I also will acknowledge before my Father in heaven;

but whoever denies me before others, I also will deny
before my Father in heaven. *(Matthew 10:32)*

Jesus is the connection of the things that are hidden in God's
foolish plan with those things that are revealed. To those who get
the connection Jesus grants peace. Those who do not get the connection see the burdens as heavy and for the rest of their lives.
Those who get the connection see being with Jesus for the rest of
their lives. Rest or rest? Do you get it?

> At that time Jesus said, "I thank you, Father, Lord of
> heaven and earth, because you have hidden these
> things from the wise and the intelligent and have
> revealed them to infants; yes, Father, for such was your
> gracious will. All things have been handed over to me
> by my Father; and no one knows the Son except the
> Father, and no one knows the Father except the Son and
> anyone to whom the Son chooses to reveal him. Come
> to me, all you that are weary and are carrying heavy
> burdens, and I will give you rest. Take my yoke upon
> you, and learn from me; for I am gentle and humble in
> heart, and you will find rest for your souls. For my yoke
> is easy, and my burden is light." *(Matthew 11:25-30)*

Jesus will be the mediator when he returns to earth again in
all his glory. He will be the judge of all nations. As Christology
developed the Church continued to confess in all three ecumenical creeds that Jesus in the mediator who will come again to
judge the living and the dead.

> When the Son of Man comes in his glory, and all the
> angels with him then he will sit on the throne of his
> glory. All the nations will be gathered before him and he
> will separate people one from another as a shepherd
> separates the sheep from the goats, and he will put the
> sheep at his right hand and the goats at the left.
> (Matthew 25:31-32)

The main form of Jesus' proclamation of his mediatorship is apocalyptic and messianic. It is divine and human sonship. Jesus in the connection, the mediator clown, between the power of God and the ideal of humility.[20]

Jesus, Servant Clown

Who is this Jesus? He is the servant clown of God. Jesus models the trans-rational values of the foolishness of God: truth over logic, giving over receiving, and serving over ruling. What a great vision of servanthood we see in Jesus. The Greek word used most often in the New Testament for "servant" or "slave" is *doulos*, perhaps the most descriptive word of a Christ clown in the New Testament.[21] This word is the key word in developing a clown ministry for Floyd Shaffer.

> The word *clod* was a term that referred to one of the lowliest members in the community: a lout, an oaf, the one set upon, the one called upon to do the work that others would not do, the lowliest of the low. Wondering if there was a similar term in New Testament Greek, I discovered that among words translated as "servant," there was one special one: *doulos*. Literally meaning "slave," this was the lowest connotation of the word translated as "servant." The *doulos* did the work that others wouldn't do and was seen as the lowliest of the low, until Jesus Christ developed the concept of servanthood.[22]

The early church saw Jesus as the servant clown of God. They understood that Jesus' servanthood was a model for all Christians. It is another descriptive picture of the foolishness of God:

---

20 Gerhard Kittel, editor, *Theological Dictionary of the New Testament* (Grand Rapids, Mich.: Eerdmans, 1967), Vol. 4, p. 621.

21 Gerhard Kittel, editor, *Theological Dictionary of the New Testament*, (Grand Rapids, Michigan: Eerdmans, 1967) Vol. 2, pp. 270-279.

22 Floyd Shaffer, *If I Were A Clown*, (Minneapolis: Augsburg Publishing House, 1984), p. 78.

Let the same mind be in you that was in Christ Jesus,
who, though he was in the form of God, did not regard
equality with God as something to be exploited, but
emptied himself, taking the form of a slave, being born
in human form, he humbled himself and became obedient to the point of death—even death on a cross.
Therefore God also high exalted him and gave him the
name that is above every name so that at the name of
Jesus every knee should bend, in heaven and on earth
and under the earth, and every tongue should confess
that Jesus Christ is Lord, to the glory of God the Father.
(Philippians 2:5-11)

The concept of Jesus as the servant clown of God is rich in
meaning. In our culture, we feel better using the term *servant*
rather than *slave*. The Civil War was fought in the United States
over the concept of slave. So often translators prefer to use the
word *servant*. But the emphasis of servanthood in Scripture is
serving as a slave. For the slave (*doulos*), service is not a matter
of choice. The servant must perform to the will of the owner. The
slave is owned and not free. The slave is totally dependent on the
master. But the good news in this concept is that the Creator God
is the master. Through the foolish act of God in the cross of
Christ, the Creator God redeemed fallen humanity and freed us
from being slaves to the devil, the world, and our flesh. We are
freed to be slaves of God. What an interesting and foolish picture! In this new relationship servanthood includes a total commitment to the Godhead. It is essential for the servant to specify
to whom the service is rendered. So the work of a servant of God
always testifies to God.[23]

As was pointed out earlier in this chapter, everything Jesus
did pointed to the Father. If we follow the call to servanthood in
Philippians 2, then everything a clown in ministry does must be

23 Gerhard Kittel, *Theological Dictionary of the New Testament, Vol. 2* (Grand
Rapids, Mich.: Eerdmans, 1967), pp. 261, 262.

in service to the Father and must acknowledge him as God and Lord.

Using the magnifying cross of Christ, we will take a close look at Jesus as the Servant of God, the slave clown through the servant songs of the Old Testament. The four servant songs are written in Deutero-Isaiah:

1. Isaiah 42:1-4
2. Isaiah 49:1-6
3. Isaiah 50:4-9
4. Isaiah 52:13—53:12

In the first servant song, Isaiah 42:1-4, it is Yahweh who introduces his servant. He gives a sign that he has chosen the servant. Yahweh anoints him with the Spirit and gives him a mission to bring forth justice:

> Here is my servant, whom I uphold, my chosen, in whom my soul delights; I have put my spirit upon him; he will bring forth justice to the nations. He will not cry or lift up his voice, or make it heard in the street; a bruised reed he will not break, and a dimly burning wick he will not quench; he will faithfully bring forth justice. He will not grow faint or be crushed until he has established justice in the earth; and the coastlands wait for his teaching. (Isaiah 42:1-4)

At the baptism of Jesus in the Synoptic Gospels (Matthew 3:13-17; Mark 1:9-11; and Luke 3:21-22) there is an obvious connection to the first servant song. It is God who introduces his

Son with the words: "This is my Son, the Beloved, with whom I am well pleased." The sign of Jesus carrying out the mission of God was his being anointed with the Holy Spirit. John's Gospel emphasizes that the Spirit descended and remained with Jesus. The New Testament Greek word for "remain" is *meno*. This word is used in John's Gospel forty times, twenty-three times in 1 John, and three times in 2 John. The concept is that of establishing an immutable and inviolable relationship.[24] John is saying, "If you are looking for the Spirit of God, keep your eyes fixed on this Jesus and live together." To be in Christ is to be in the Spirit:

> And John testified, "I saw the Spirit descending from heaven like a dove, and it remained on him. I myself did not know him, but the one who sent me to baptize with water said to me, 'He on whom you see the Spirit descend and remain is the one who baptizes with the Holy Spirit.' And I myself have seen and have testified that this is the Son of God." *(John 1:32-34)*

The connection of the Spirit of God with Jesus becomes a theme for Luke in his writing of Luke/Acts. In Luke the theme is "Jesus led by the Spirit." Luke mentions in the birth narrative that the child, Jesus, will be holy because he is of the Holy Spirit:

> The angel said to her, "The Holy Spirit will come upon you, and the power of the Most High will overshadow you; therefore the child to be born will be holy; he will be called Son of God." *(Luke 1:35)*

> Jesus, full of the Holy Spirit, returned from the Jordan and was led by the Spirit in the wilderness, where for forty days he was tempted by the devil. (Luke 4:1, 2)

> Then Jesus, filled with the power of the Spirit, returned

---

24 Gerhard Kittel, editor, *Theological Dictionary of the New Testament* (Grand Rapids, Mich.: Eerdmans, 1967), Vol. 4, pp. 574-576.

to Galilee, and a report about him spread through all
the surrounding county. (Luke 4:14)

Luke's theme in writing Acts is "The church of Jesus Christ
led by the Spirit." The book of Acts might better have been enti-
tled The Acts of the Spirit rather than The Acts of the Apostles.
Luke begins the Gospel with mentioning that the actions in this
book are through the Holy Spirit (Acts 1:2), then he tells of
Jesus' words to the disciples about being baptized with the Holy
Spirit (Acts 1:5). In Acts 2 is the outpouring of the Holy Spirit on
Pentecost. In Acts 10 Peter also connects Jesus to the Servant of
God in his conversation with Cornelius:

> How God anointed Jesus of Nazareth with the Holy
> Spirit and with power; how he went about doing good
> and healing all who were oppressed by the devil, for
> God was with him. (Acts 10:38)

In the birth narrative in the Gospel of Matthew, Matthew
notes that Mary will conceive a child from the Holy Spirit
(Matthew 1:20). Mark begins his Gospel with the baptism of
Jesus and thus connects Jesus to the first servant song.

In the second servant song, Isaiah 49:1-6, the servant
announces himself as called by Yahweh from his birth for a mission of Yahweh. Yahweh named him. He is to be a light to the
nations that Yahweh's salvation may reach the end of the earth:

> Listen to me, O coastlands, pay attention, you peoples
> from far away! The Lord called me before I was born,
> while I was in my mother's womb he named me. He
> made my mouth like a sharp sword, in the shadow of his
> hand he hid me; he made me a polished arrow, in his
> quiver he hid me away. And he said to me, "You are my
> servant, Israel, in whom I will be glorified," But I said, "I
> have labored in vain, I have spent my strength for noth-
> ing and vanity; yet surely my cause is with the Lord, and

my reward with my God" And now the Lord says, who
formed me in the womb to be his servant, to bring Jacob
back to him, for I am honored in the sight of the Lord,
and my God has become my strength—he says, "it is too
light a thing that you should be my servant to raise up
the tribes of Jacob and to restore the survivors of Israel;
I will give you as a light to the nations, that my salvation
may reach to the end of the earth." *(Isaiah 49:1-6)*

The birth narratives in the Synoptic Gospels connect Jesus
with the second servant song. Jesus is born of a woman and God
names him:

And now, you will conceive in your womb and bear a
son, and you will name him Jesus. *(Luke 1:31)*

She will bear a son, and you are to name him Jesus, for
he will save his people from their sins. *(Matthew 1:21)*

His name, "Jesus," is his mission—"deliverance." In the
song of Simeon, Jesus is seen as the deliverer and the light to the
Gentiles of the second servant song:

For my eyes have seen your salvation, which you have
prepared in the presence of all peoples, a light for revelation to the Gentiles and for glory to your people Israel.
(Luke 2:31-32)

Luke keeps this interest of the Gentile mission going
throughout the book of Acts.

Then both Paul and Barnabas spoke out boldly, saying,
"It was necessary that the word of God should be spoken first to you. Since you reject it and judge yourselves
to be unworthy of eternal life, we are now turning to
the Gentiles. For so the Lord has commanded us, saying,
'I have set you to be a light for the Gentiles, so that you

may bring salvation to the ends of the earth.'"
(Acts 13:46, 47)

In the third servant song, Isaiah 50:4-9, the servant describes a relationship to Yahweh. There is an emphasis of daily obedience and an outrageous response:

The Lord God has given me the tongue of a teacher, that
I may know how to sustain the weary with a word.
Morning by morning he wakens—wakens my ear to
listen as those who are taught. The Lord God has
opened my ear, and I was not rebellious, I did not turn
backward. I gave my back to those who struck me, and
my cheeks to those who pulled out the beard; I did not
hide my face from insult and spitting. The Lord God
helps me; therefore I have not been disgraced; therefore
I have set my face like flint, and I know that I shall not
be put to shame; he who vindicates me is near. Who will
contend with me? Let us stand up together. Who are my
adversaries? Let them confront me. It is the Lord God
who helps me; who will declare me guilty? All of them
will wear out like a garment; the moth will eat them up.
(Isaiah 50:4-9)

The connection with the third servant song is with Jesus' relationship with the Father. Obediently, Jesus does his Father's will. In Luke 2, Jesus reminds Joseph and Mary of his servant mission:

He said to them, "Why were you searching for me? Did
you not know that I must be in my Father's house?"
(Luke 2:49)

Jesus, knowing the outrageous abuse in his coming crucifixion, prays at the Mount of Olives that, if it is possible, this coming suffering be removed. But Jesus goes to the cross and is obedient to the will of the Father.

And going a little farther, he threw himself on the ground and prayed, "My Father, if it is possible, let this cup pass from me; yet not what I want but what you want." *(Matthew 26:39)*

Again he went away for the second time and prayed, "My Father, if this cannot pass unless I drink it, your will be done." *(Matthew 26:42)*

(Also compare Mark 14:36 and Luke 22:42)

The fourth servant song, Isaiah 52:13—53:12, is much too long for me to print in this book. But I encourage you to read it. As a personal spiritual discipline, read this servant song each day during the forty days of Lent. It describes the servant clown of God, Jesus, enduring the grief of the sins of all people. In the fourth servant song, the suffering servant was shown as the means by which the servant would complete the mission of Yahweh. The section of the suffering servant is introduced with language that anticipates a final triumph.[25] The following are some selected verses from the fourth servant song:

He was despised and rejected by others; a man of suffering and acquainted with infirmity. *(Isaiah 53:3)*

Surely he has borne our infirmities and carried our diseases; yet we accounted him stricken, struck down by God and afflicted. But he was wounded for our transgressions, crushed for our iniquities; upon him was the punishment that made us whole and by his bruises we are healed. All we like sheep have gone astray; we have all turned to our own way, and the Lord has laid on him the iniquity of us all. (Isaiah 53:4-6)

25 George Buttrick, editor, *The Interpreter's Dictionary of the Bible*, (New York: Abingdon Press, 1962), Vol. 4, pp. 292, 293.

The fourth servant song is seen in the passion narratives in the Gospels. Each of the four Gospels shows Jesus as the suffering Servant of God (Matthew 26–27; Mark 14–15; Luke 22–23; John 18–19). Nowhere in Scripture is the foolish plan of God more visible than in the suffering and death of Jesus, the Christ. Who would have seen God accomplishing his purpose through the cross?[26]

In Acts 3 Peter's sermon in the temple area declares Jesus as the Servant of God:

> The God of Abraham, and of Isaac, and the God of Jacob, the God of our ancestors has glorified his servant, Jesus, whom you handed over and rejected in the presence of Pilate, though he had decided to release him. But you rejected the Holy and Righteous One and asked to have a murderer given to you. *(Acts 3:13-14)*

In the account of Philip and the Ethiopian in Acts 8, Philip helps the Ethiopian understand the meaning of the suffering servant in Isaiah 53:7 by telling him of Jesus.

> Now the passage of the scripture that he was reading was this: "Like a sheep he was led to the slaughter, and like a lamb silent before its shearer, so he does not open his mouth. In his humiliation justice was denied him. Who can describe his generation? For his life is taken away from the earth." The eunuch asked Philip, "About whom, may I ask you, does the prophet say this, about himself or about someone else?" Then Philip began to speak, and starting with this scripture, he proclaimed to him the good news about Jesus. *(Acts 8:32-35)*

Before the crucifixion, Jesus in Luke 22:37 makes reference to the fourth servant song with the words:

---

26 Gerhard Kittel, editor, *Theological Dictionary of the New Testament* (Grand Rapids, Mich.: Eerdmans, 1967), Vol. 5, pp. 700-704.

For I tell you, this scripture must be fulfilled in me. "And he was counted among the lawless"; and indeed what is written about me is being fulfilled.

New Testament scholar F. F. Bruce in *New Testament Development of Old Testament Themes*, quotes C. H. Dodd in reference to Jesus being the Servant of God described in the songs of Isaiah:

To account for the beginning of this most original and fruitful process of re-thinking the Old Testament we found need to postulate a creative mind. The Gospels offers us one. Are we compelled to reject the offer?[27]

F. F. Bruce argues in favor of Jesus being understood as the suffering servant of the songs of Isaiah. He states and discusses four propositions:

1. Jesus spoke of himself as the Son of Man.
2. Jesus spoke of the suffering Son of Man.
3. Jesus spoke of the Son of Man's suffering as something that was written.
4. Jesus spoke of the Son of Man's suffering as a "ransom for many."

Each of these propositions, Bruce argues, shows that Jesus was the Servant of God described in the songs of Isaiah.[28]

In Luke 4 Jesus picked up the scroll of the prophet Isaiah, read the first few verses from Isaiah 61, put the scroll aside, and said to the people that he fulfilled the prophecy of Isaiah. The people were amazed and asked one of the questions of Christology: "Who is this Jesus?"

And he rolled up the scroll, gave it back to the attendant, and sat down. The eyes of all in the synagogue

27 F. F. Bruce, *The New Testament Development of Old Testament Themes* (Grand Rapids, Mich.: Eerdmans, 1968), p. 97. The reference noted is C. H. Dodd, *According to the Scriptures*, (London, 1952), p. 110.

28 F. F. Bruce, *The New Testament Development of Old Testament Themes*, pp. 97-99.

were fixed on him. Then he began to say to them,
"Today this scripture has been fulfilled in your hearing."
All spoke well of him and were amazed at the gracious
words that came from his mouth. They said, "Is not this
Joseph's son?" *(Luke 4:20-22)*

Beholding Jesus through the Old Testament servant songs of
Isaiah, the clown learns that a Servant God wants a servant people. We give glory to our God by taking the lowliest roles in society and faithfully doing the lowliest tasks. Jesus not only mentioned this to the 12 disciples, the greater number of followers,
and the crowds, but he modeled it as a way of life. A Christ clown
is a servant of God for life and is totally dedicated to God.

In the circus a clown may be working hard on the carpet of
the hippodrome to bring laughter to the audience one minute and
the next minute may be wearing coveralls and carrying a shovel
and following behind the elephants. The Christ clown will give
up self to help others see Christ.

I know that reading through this section on Jesus as the servant clown of God is the most difficult section of this book
because I have included so much detail about the servant songs
of Isaiah. I pray that you will read this carefully and often to see
the clear connections of Isaiah signs of the Messiah and Jesus.
For if clowns in ministry of the gospel are to have the mind of
Christ as in Philippians 2, then those clowns must know exactly
what this is. This is not a novelty. It is a ministry to the glory of
God. Servanthood does not draw attention to or reward the costume and makeup of the servant. The servanthood of Christ only
points to the Father.

Jesus had total commitment to the will of the Father. He
showed how one could worship God as a way of life. His commitment to the will of the Father caused him to look at people in
a different light, the light of love. Jesus showed that through servanthood one proclaims the kingdom of God. Jesus emptied himself and gave up all authority to serve others with love. Rather

than using power, Jesus empowers people with love. This selfless serving of others with love is the sign of the servant clown, Jesus.

Christ clowns are to have the same mind in them that was in Christ Jesus. Christ clowns are to serve all the way to the cross and empty tomb. The New Testament Greek word used most often for "ministry" is *diakonia*, from which we get the English word *deacon*. *Diakonia* literally means waiting at table.[29] Another New Testament Greek word used for "ministry" is *leitourgia,* from which we get the English word *liturgy*.[30] With the same mind as Christ, the servant clown of God, clowns in ministry serve the common needs of other people so that they see God. Christ clowns can also serve in worship to help people see God. Everything a Christ clown does should give witness to the foolish plan of our gracious God.

Jesus, Interpreter Clown

In his ministry, Jesus was always on the move from town to town through Galilee, Judea, and even Samaria. Jesus moved close to people because faith is formed by the Holy Spirit through personal relationships. Jesus is moved by compassion and the target of his love is people.

In the late 19th century a new clown type emerged with the hobo or tramp clown. The tramp clown symbolized the people whose lives were always on the move from city to city. They carried with them, perhaps one suitcase, a knapsack, or a homemade carrying case crafted from a large handkerchief tied to a stick.[31]

Clowns working in ministry today often use a suitcase as a symbol that ministry must move. The movement is always from person to person. Jesus the clown on the move, is seen as the interpreter of the kingdom of God.

This is a role that the court fool used to play. The court fool

29 Gerhard Kittel, editor, Theological Dictionary of the New Testament, (Grand Rapids, Michigan: Eerdemans, 1967) Vol. 2, p 87.

30 Fredrick W. Danker and F. Wilbur Gingrich, *Shorter Lexicon of the Greek New Testament* (Chicago: University of Chicago Press, 1983), p. 117.

31 John H. Towsen, *Clowns* (New York: Hawthorn Books, Inc., 1976), pp. 282-305.

would interpret the events of the kingdom and both the relationship of the king to the people and the people to the king. Often
the antics of the court fool would challenge the politics and
social action of the kingdom.[32] By interpreting the kingdom of
God, Jesus challenged people to look carefully again at religion
and the practice of religion.

Jesus used parables to interpret the kingdom of heaven to
people. The parables ask questions of Christology: "Who is this
Jesus? Do I believe this? How will I live this?" Even though each
parable may have a different point, the same questions of Christology are asked. If people do not answer those three questions,
they will not understand the parable. Belief in Jesus as the
Messiah is the key to understanding the parables of the kingdom.
The parables lead people to Jesus. Then faith seeks understanding of the kingdom.

> Jesus told the crowds all these things in parables; with-
> out a parable he told them nothing. This was to fulfill
> what had been spoken through the prophet: "I will open
> my mouth to speak in parables; I will proclaim what has
> been hidden from the foundation of the world."
> (Matthew 13:34-35)

Jesus, like a court jester, moves among the people to interpret the kingdom and the meaning of faith with his healing miracles. Much like a clown, sometimes he heals before a large
crowd of people, and other times before only a few people.
Whether calming a storm, giving sight to the blind, enabling the
lame to walk, freeing people from demons, or raising the dead,
Jesus shows that he is the way, the truth, and the life. Faith centers in the person and presence of Jesus. Jesus is the key to interpreting the kingdom of God.

> The law and the prophets were in effect until John came;
> since then the good news of the kingdom of God is pro-

32 John H. Towsen, *Clowns*, pp. 21-30.

claimed, and everyone tries to enter it by force. But it is
easier for heaven and earth to pass away, than for one
stoke of a letter in the law to be dropped. *(Luke 16:16)*

Jesus is saying that without a gospel interpreter, people will
not understand the kingdom of God or see the key to being in and
of the kingdom of God. What follows in Luke 16 is a parable
about the rich man and Lazarus, a poor man. Jesus concludes in
Luke 16:31:

He said to him, "If they do not listen to Moses and the
prophets, neither will they be convinced even if someone rises from the dead."

If people do not deal with the Christological question "Who
is this Jesus?" then they will not understand or enter the kingdom
of God.

Jesus interprets the meaning of the law of the Sabbath in
Luke 6. Like a clown or a court jester, Jesus spoofs traditional
views that have not led people to the point:

One Sabbath while Jesus was going through the grain-
fields, his disciples plucked some heads of grain, rubbed
them in their hands, and ate them. But some of the
Pharisees said, "Why are you doing what is not lawful
on the Sabbath?" Jesus answered, "Have you not read
what David did when he and his companions were hungry? He entered the house of God and took and ate the
bread of the Presence, which it is not lawful for any but
the priest to eat, and gave some to his companions?"
Then he said to them, "The Son of Man is lord of the
Sabbath." *(Luke 6:1-5)*

Earlier in this chapter we have noted how Jesus in the
Sermon on the Mount (Matthew 5—9) brings a new interpretation to the law with the phrase, "You've heard it said…but I tell
you." The key to this new understanding of the law is Jesus.

Do not think that I have come to abolish the law or the
prophets; I have come not to abolish but to fulfill.
(Matthew 5:17)

We do not enter the kingdom of God through our own efforts.
In the Sermon on the Mount Jesus shows how all of us fall short
of perfection and that all of us are sinful. But through Jesus, the
fulfiller of the law, we can enter the kingdom of heaven.

Jesus again points to himself as the key to understanding the
kingdom of God in a discussion with some Pharisees. The
Pharisees didn't get it.

Once Jesus was asked by the Pharisees when the kingdom of God was coming, and he answered, "The kingdom of God is not coming with things that can be
observed; nor will they say, 'Look, here it is!' or 'There it
is!' For, in fact, the kingdom of God is among you."
(Luke 17:20-21)

In an argument over who is the greatest in the kingdom of
God by some of the disciples, Jesus takes a child and gives a new
interpretation of the kingdom of God. In doing so he shares a
new value of children and surprises his disciples and others in the
crowd. I don't think there could be a more powerful affirmation
of the ministry of a clown than this interpretation. Because
clowns value children, they minister to children of all ages.

People were bringing even infants to him that he might
touch them; and when the disciples saw it, they sternly
ordered them not to do it. But Jesus called for them and
said, "Let the little children come to me, and do not stop
them; for it is to such as these that the kingdom of God
belongs. Truly I tell you, whoever does not receive the
kingdom of God as a little child will never enter it."
(Luke 18:15-17)

(Also compare Matthew 18:1-7 and Mark 9:33-37)

When Jesus provides a clear meaning of Messiah by pointing to the cross, the disciples did not get it and wanted Jesus to stop giving that interpretation.

> The he began to teach them that the Son of Man must undergo great suffering, and be rejected by the elders, the chief priests, and the scribes, and be killed, and after three days rise again. He said all this quite openly. And Peter took him aside and began to rebuke him. But turning and looking at his disciples, he rebuked Peter and said, "Get behind me, Satan! For you are setting your mind not on divine things but on human things."
> *(Mark 9:31-33)*

Immediately following this interpretation of Messiah, Jesus interprets what it means to be a follower of Jesus. This interpretation again affirms the foolishness of God's plan of salvation and living in the kingdom of God. Because the kingdom of God is among us now, a follower of Jesus will take great risks to be faithful:

> He called the crowd with his disciples, and said to them, "If any want to become my followers, let them deny themselves and take up their cross and follow me. For those who want to save their life will lose it, and those who lose their life for my sake and for the sake of the gospel, will save it. For what will it profit them to gain the whole world and forfeit their life?" *(Mark 9:34-37)*
> *(Also compare Luke 9:23-27)*

Jesus' interpretation of how difficult it is for a rich person to enter the kingdom of God provides one of my favorite clown routines. Jesus, the interpreter clown, provides a hilarious picture:

> Then Jesus looked around and said to his disciples, "How hard it will be for those who have wealth to enter the kingdom of God!" And the disciples were perplexed

at these words. But Jesus said to them again, "Children, how hard it is to enter the kingdom of God! It is easier for a camel to go through the eye of a needle than for someone who is rich to enter the kingdom of God." *(Mark 10:23-25)*

Jesus continues to serve as the interpreter as he lives with his disciples. With his disciples, other followers, and outcasts Jesus interprets the kingdom of God by pointing to what surrounds the people and showing them what was always there—the hidden grace and love of God. He points out something from their common life and says, "The kingdom of God is like this...." Clowns in ministry learn from Jesus' interpretation that the central focus of all clown ministry is the death and resurrection of Jesus. They also learn from Jesus that they do not have to bring a trailer full of props. It is best to use what surrounds the people and help them see the presence of a God who loves them.

After the resurrection, Jesus still is the interpreter clown. In Luke 24, on the road to Emmaus, Jesus interprets the Scriptures to the two men walking along the road. When they meet Jesus on the road, the two men do not recognize him. Jesus connects the role of Messiah with his life, death, and resurrection. His resurrected presence was the focal point to understanding the Scriptures.

Then beginning with Moses and all the prophets, he interpreted to them the things in all the scriptures. As they came near the village to which they were going, he walked ahead as if he were going on. But they urged him strongly, saying, "Stay with us, because it is almost evening and the day is now nearly over." So he went in to stay with them. When he was at the table with them, he took bread, blessed and broke it, and gave it to them. Then their eyes were opened, and they recognized him, and he vanished from their sight. They said to each other, "Were not our hearts burning within us while he was talking to us on the road, while he was opening the scriptures to us?" *(Luke 24:27-32)*

In the last chapters of both Matthew and Luke, Jesus interprets his resurrection to his disciples and followers in terms of they being witnesses. They are to proclaim that the promise of God has been fulfilled in Jesus (Matthew 28; Luke 24).

Jesus, Corporate Clown

The Scriptures indicate that Jesus offered more than his name or a recollection of his teaching to his disciples. It was not a $15 compact disc of Jesus' greatest hits that made the disciples into bold witnesses of the gospel. Rather, it was the resurrected presence of Jesus himself that empowered them. As was written earlier, if a person is looking for the power of the Holy Spirit, she should keep her eyes fixed on Jesus, the Christ. It was the resurrected presence of Jesus that caused Thomas to express, "My Lord and my God!" (John 20:28). It was the presence of Jesus that caused Mary Magdalene to proclaim, "I have seen the Lord," and to witness to the other disciples (John 20:18). It was Jesus' presence that warmed the hearts of the two disciples on the road to Emmaus (Luke 24:32). His presence caused Peter to jump into the water and run to the shore to be with Jesus (John 21:7). Jesus offers his presence as his promise for life with God. It is the promise of his presence that enables the body of Christ, the church, to carry out the mission, the foolish plan of God.

> And Jesus came and said to them, "All authority in heaven and on earth has been given to me. Go therefore and make disciples of all nations, baptizing them in the name of the Father and of the Son and of the Holy Spirit, and teaching them to obey everything that I have commanded you. And remember, I am with you always, to the end of the age." *(Matthew 28:19-20)*

Jesus offers an intimate relationship with God through his

presence, an incorporation. C. F. D. Moule uses a major portion
of his book, *The Origin of Christology*, to develop an understanding and experience of Christ as corporate. Moule states that
the understanding of Christ as corporate is undeniably early and
well established.[33]

To be in the body of Christ, the church is to be in union with
Christ and in union with the members themselves. Two concepts of
the church as the people of God and the body of Christ are different ways of expressing our union with God through Christ and our
union with one another through the same redemptive act of Christ.

> The Church is only the body of Christ insofar as it is the
> people of God; but by being the new people of God con-
> stituted by Christ it is truly the body of Christ.[34]

The concept of the body of Christ as the church is used in the
New Testament writings attributed to Paul. Paul emphasizes two
different ideas of the body of Christ. In Romans 12 and 1
Corinthians 12, Paul uses the term *body of Christ* in reference to
the local community of believers as the body of Christ. In
Ephesians and Colossians, *body of Christ* means the whole
church. Both of these unions happen through the redemptive act
of Christ Jesus.

In 1 Corinthians 12 and Romans 12 the members of the body
of Christ are people with a variety of gifts. In both these chapters
the emphasis is on the relationship of the members to one another. They are to be living out the foolish mission of God so that
others see a God who loves them. The description is not of individual members grafted to the head, Jesus. But rather they are
connected to each other. In baptism we are totally immersed into
Christ's death and resurrection and our differences become gifts
of the body of Christ. It is an important picture of the church that
is so misunderstood.

33 C. F. D. Moule, *The Origin of Christology* (Cambridge: Cambridge University
   Press, 1977), pp. 47-96.
34 Hans Kung, *The Church* (New York: Sheed and Ward, 1967), p. 225.

By linking his teaching about charismata with that about the body of Christ, Paul at all events made clear that the church is never—as some people in Corinth seem to have supposed—a gathering of charismatics enjoying their own private relationship with Christ independently of the community. [35]

The emphasis of Jesus as corporate clown is on the third question of Christology, "How do I live this faith?" In Romans 12 and 1 Corinthians 12, Paul is concerned about how the members of the body of Christ get along with one another using their different gifts to the glory of God. There should be no feelings, expressions, or displays of superiority among members.

For by the grace given to me I say to everyone among you not to think of yourself more highly than you ought to think, but to think with sober judgment, each according to the measure of faith that God has assigned. For as in one body we have many members, and not all the members have the same function, so we, who are many, are one body in Christ, individually, we are members of one another. *(Romans 12:3-5)*

But God has so arranged the body, giving the greater honor to the inferior member, that there may be no dissension within the body, but the members may have the same care for one another. If one member suffers, all suffer together with it; if one member is honored, all rejoice together with it. *(1 Corinthians 12:24-26)*

It is only through Christ that we have this union with God and with one another.

The message of Paul is always founded in the grace of God, God's foolish plan.

35 Hans Kung, *The Church*, p. 227.

Paul's view of the Church as the body of Christ presents
an imperative which is founded on an indicative. Because
the believers, through baptism and in the Spirit, are members of the body of Christ, because through the Lord's
Supper they are united in one body, then they ought in
their everyday lives to live as members of the body and
realize the unity of the one body. The body of Christ is not
the result of the efforts of individual members of the
community, who have formed themselves together into
one body and thereby, through their love and desire for
unity, constitute the body of Christ. The body of Christ has
been constituted by Christ and in this sense pre-exists.[36]

In Ephesians and Colossians the concern of the body of
Christ is not their relationship to one another, but the relationship
of the body to the head, Christ. The church is subject to Christ.
In these two epistles, to be in relationship with Christ is the goal
of the mission of the church.

But speaking the truth in love, we must grow up in
every way into him who is the head, into Christ, from
whom the whole body, joined and knit together by every
ligament with which it is equipped, as each part is
working properly, promotes the body's growth in building itself up in love. (Ephesians 4:15-16) (Compare
Colossians 1:18; 2:19)

He is the image of the invisible God, the firstborn of all
creation; for in him all things in heaven and on earth
were created, things visible and invisible, whether
thrones or dominions or rulers or powers—all things
have been created through him and for him. He himself
is before all things, and in him all things hold together.
He is the head of the body, the church, he is the beginning, the firstborn from the dead, so that he might come

36 Hans Kung, *The Church*, p. 229.

to have first place in everything. For in him all the fullness of God was pleased to dwell, and through him God
was pleased to reconcile to himself all things, whether
on earth or in heaven, by making peace through the
blood of his cross. *(Colossians 1:15-20)*

The incorporate phrases in Christ (*en Christo*) and in the
Lord (*en Kurio*) used throughout the New Testament shows that
Jesus is the focal point for an intimate relationship with God. It
is baptism into Christ that brings new life:

Do you not know that all of us who have been baptized
into Christ Jesus were baptized into his death? Therefore
we have been buried with him by baptism into death, so
that, just as Christ was raised from the dead by the
glory of the Father, so we too might walk in newness of
life. *(Romans 6:3-4)*

When a person is *in Christ*, that believer is also in the Spirit
of God. Note the action of baptism and the emphasis on baptism
as being a way of life. Again, Jesus, the corporate clown, brings
us to the third question of Christology: "How do I live this faith?"

And this is what some of you used to be. But you were
washed, you were sanctified, you were justified in the
name of the Lord Jesus Christ and in the Spirit of our
God. *(1 Corinthians 6:11)*

But you are not in the flesh; you are in the Spirit, since
the Spirit of God dwells in you. Anyone who does not
have the Spirit of Christ does not belong to him. But if
Christ is in you, though the body is dead because of sin,
the Spirit is life because of righteousness. If the Spirit of
him who raised Jesus from the dead dwells in you, he
who raised Christ from the dead will give life to your
mortal bodies also through his Spirit that dwells in you.
(Romans 8:9-11)

When a person is baptized into Christ, that person is baptized into the body of Christ:

> Doubtless it is impossible to contemplate being baptized into Christ without being baptized into the Body, but the Body must be defined in terms of Christ, not vice versa. If we appeal to the concept of corporate personality, it is Christ who is the "inclusive personality" and who informs the members with His character. He does not receive his nature from them. The Church is subject to Christ in all things, including its very life.[37]

In baptism, Jesus, the corporate clown, brings us into a relationship with God and with one another. To be in Christ means to *put on* Christ. Christ is to be visible in everything that we do.

> As many of you as were baptized into Christ have clothed yourselves with Christ. *(Galatians 3:27)*

The imagery of a clown putting on the makeup and costume is very helpful in understanding this. The presence of Jesus affects how we look and how we live. It is not simply knowing about Jesus, but being in Christ, that causes us to put on Christ. Herb Brokering has written a wonderful parable in a book entitled *The Wet Walk* about being in Christ, or *en Christo.*

> Once there was a people who were very bored with a very important idea, *en Christo.* They were educated but were not very wise. They knew it meant in Christ, but they did not have the idea inside their lives. So they watched their children to find the answer. They saw them get into trees, into barrels, into big tires, into sand, into boxes, and into water. So the people moved into everything of Christ with the imagination of their children. Whatever Christ has was their own. They got into his birth as though Mary

37 G. R. Beasley-Murry, *Baptism in the New Testament* (London: MacMillan & Co., 1963), p. 171.

was their own mother; into his life as though they were in the boat and unafraid, into the hillside as though they had all that bread and fish, into the water as though the Holy Spirit was over them and into Christ's grave as though resurrection was theirs. Sometimes they covered themselves with special garments to get into Christ, as their children taught them. They were surprised by the large amount of room they found in Christ. The more they got into, the more the space increased. *En Christo* is something they are all into.[38]

The symbol of the clown is a helpful tool of Christology to understand who this Jesus is as corporate clown. The clown in ministry, or Christ clown, literally puts on Christ. Clown alley for Christian clowns is a sacred space. For this is the time when they get into Christ. The clown face is not a mask. Rather, it is a tool to communicate the unique characteristics of a specific clown living life inside-out. The clown face, character, and costume should express being in Christ. The white grease paint is a symbol of death.

The clown's historic makeup is a symbol of death and resurrection. The white is the symbol of death and is applied first. The colors symbolize life. Thus, a clown's face is a reminder that we are on a journey from death to life; it constitutes the reality of Easter.[39]

---

38 Herb Brokering, *The Wet Walk* (St. Louis, Mo.: Concordia Publishing House, 1976), p. 8.

39 Floyd Shaffer and Penne Sewall, *Clown Ministry* (Loveland, Colo.: Group Books, 1984), p. 14.

While putting on make-up, the clown is reminded that in Christ we are dead to sin. Our sins die on the cross. So putting on the make up can actually be an act of confession and absolution. It is sin and grace, law and gospel, death and resurrection. While putting on the white grease paint, the clown can think of all his or her personal sins that died on the cross. The bright colors of the clown face represent the brightness of living life in an intimate relationship with God and with the people of God. So while the clown puts on the colors, she may think of all the things that she is alive to. Martin Luther, in his Small Catechism, expressed so well what it means to be dead to sin and alive to God:

WHAT DOES SUCH BAPTIZING WITH WATER SIGNIFY?
ANSWER: It signifies that the old Adam in us, together with all sins and evil lusts, should be drowned by daily sorrow and repentance and be put to death, so that the new man should come forth daily and rise up, cleansed and righteous, to live forever in God's presence.

WHERE IS THIS WRITTEN?
ANSWER: In Romans 6:4, St. Paul wrote, "We were buried therefore with him by baptism into death, so that as Christ was raised from the dead by the glory of the Father, we too might walk in the newness of life."[40]

---

40 Theodore Tappert, editor, The Book of Concord (St. Louis, Mo.: Concordia Publishing House, 1959), p. 349. Luther's Small Catechism, published in 1529, was included in the Book of Concord of 1580.

In her book, *The Clown Ministry Handbook*, Janet Litherland also expresses how the clown helps people see death and new life in themselves:

> Through love, the clown helps us, also, to "die" a little, so that our lives may be filled with better things. There is a lot of love in the world, but too few are able to express it, particularly with "no strings attached" kind of love.[41]

> "Love so amazing, so divine
> Demands my soul, my life my all."[42]

Christology is the heart of clown ministry. The clown who puts on Christ celebrates with joy the common, ordinary, routine, dull, and even the boring of every day, knowing the certainty of the presence of the risen Christ. In Christ the clown is no longer captivated by fear of the weaknesses of humanity, but freed to move among people to share the foolish plan of God. In Christ the clown is a forgiven fool. In Christ the clown is part of a body that lives the gospel. The clown can even accept death and plant tears because the clown knows resurrection in Christ.

In an intimate relationship with God, the clown moves among people. Much like a parable in the Gospels, the clown points to Jesus and raises the questions:

1. Who is this Jesus?
2. Do I believe this?
3. How do I live this faith?

41 Janet Litherland, *The Clown Ministry Handbook* (Colorado Springs, Colo.: Meriwether Publishing, Ltd., 1982), p.13.

42 From the last line of the fourth verse of the hymn "When I Survey the Wondrous Cross," text written by Isaac Watts (1674-1748).

A Theology with Clown Types

Over the past 28 years that I have been involved in clown ministry I have noticed that each of the three basic types of clowns—whiteface, auguste, and tramp—focuses on a more specific area of theology. No matter what type of clown, all clowns in ministry create word pictures of the gospel of Jesus Christ. They point people to Christ and raise the Christological questions: "Who is this Jesus? Do I believe this? How then will I live this?" All clowns in ministry are like teeter-totters that connect and balance sin and grace, law and gospel, and death and resurrection. All Christian clowns are dead to sin, but alive to God, and walk in the newness of life. But the various clown types give us a different emphasis in theology. In this chapter we will take a close look at the unique theological emphasis of each clown type.

The Tramp Clown

Remember that you are dust, and to dust you shall return.[1]

The ancient custom of using ashes to make the sign of the cross on a person's forehead on the first day of Lent is a powerful symbol of the church. Symbols are important not in themselves, but for the story behind them. The ashes and the sign of the cross not only remind us of our humanity but also tell us the story of our

---

1 From the imposition of ashes in the Ash Wednesday liturgy. *Lutheran Book of Worship Minister's Desk Edition* (Minneapolis: Augsburg Publishing House), 1978, page 131.

journey. It is a story of dead and alive, of Good Friday and Easter, of sin and grace. It is a story of what life is all about!

Ashes, in a Jewish and Christian context suggest judgment and God's condemnation of sin (Genesis 3:19), frailty, our total dependence upon God for life (Psalm 90:3; 104:29; Ecclesiastes 3:20 and 12:7), humiliation (Genesis 18:27; Esther 4:1; Jonah 3:6; 2 Samuel 13:19; Daniel 9:3), and repentance (Job 2:8; 42:6; Matthew 11:21; Luke 10:13). We are reminded forcefully of the words of the committal in the burial service, "…earth to earth, ashes to ashes, dust to dust." For one day those words will be said over us[2].

As the ashes remind us of our humanity, so does the clown. We are people who trip, fall, and stumble on our own. We are totally dependent on a gracious God who loves us despite our fallen state. God stoops down in Jesus, the Christ, forgives us and picks us up. This same gracious God calls us to live life in grace to the fullest. The Christ clown understands what or who gives life.

Of the three basic clown types (whiteface, auguste, tramp), the tramp clown best symbolizes the focus of Lent. Lent is not a season that the church plays "Let pretend that we do not know that Jesus, the Christ, was raised from the dead." Rather it is a time of ashes and sackcloth because we do know that Christ is risen. Lent is a purple time of passionate pondering on the cross of Jesus Christ. It is a time of asking, "What does this mean to me?" It is looking at the cross from the angle of our fallen humanity and listening to the Holy Spirit whisper, "I love you! You are mine! Given and shed for you!" The tramp clown lives each day dressed in sackcloth and is very

2 Philip H. Pfatteicher and Carlos R. Messerli, *Manual on the Liturgy, Lutheran Book of Worship* (Minneapolis: Augsburg Publishing House, 1979), page 307.

focused on his sin, his own sin, his own most grievous sin. The tramp clown knows the pain, suffering, and loneliness of sin, death, and the devil. The tramp is well acquainted with the evils of poverty, abuse, war, apathy, narcissism, hunger, lack of job, racism, sexism, and other injustices. The tramp clown has walked through the valley of the shadow of death, through the demons of personal and community abuses such has drugs, alcohol, pornography, power, greed, and types of exploitation.

St. Paul describes the ministry of a tramp clown so well in 2 Corinthians 4:7-12:

> But we have this treasure in clay jars, so that it may be made clear that this extraordinary power belongs to God and does not come from us. We are afflicted in every way, but not crushed; perplexed, but not driven to despair; persecuted, but not forsaken; struck down, but not destroyed; always carrying in the body the death of Jesus, so that the life of Jesus may also be made visible in our bodies. For while we live, we are always being given up to death for Jesus' sake, so that the life of Jesus may be made visible in our mortal flesh. So death is at work in us, but life in you.

Steeped in the hopelessness of our sinful nature, the tramp clown is not hopeless because the clown does not play "Let's pretend." The tramp is a reality of a fallen humanity. But because the tramp knows Easter, the clown walks through the darkness into God's marvelous light. The tramp draws no attention to self, but rather lives in the background of life. This clown reaches out to the people on the fringes, barely holding on to life. The tramp clown's costume and sad face show the effects of living with people on the fringes of life. Often with a sad face, dressed in a sackcloth costume and ashes, the people on the fringes can see this clown understands life from their viewpoint. The tramp knows of their afflictions, then points to the cross, and raises the question to the people living on the fringes of life, "What does this mean?" Just raising the question is a sign of hope and light. The tramp knows that the breathing out of a sigh—"Aah!"— is the first step of healing.

Again, it is described so well in 2 Corinthians 1:3-7:

> Blessed be the God and Father of our Lord Jesus Christ, the Father of mercies and the God of all consolation, who consoles us in all our affliction, so that we may be able to console those who are in any affliction with the consolation with which we ourselves are consoled by God. For just as the sufferings of Christ are abundant for us, so also our consolation is abundant through Christ. If we are being afflicted, it is for your consolation and salvation; if we are being consoled, it is for your consolation, which you experience when you patiently endure the same suffering. Our hope for you is unshaken; for we know that as you share in our sufferings, so also you share in our consolation.

In the Old Testament ashes and sackcloth were symbols of cleansing and renewal. The tramp clown is a symbol of confession and absolution and of the grace of baptism. The clown remembers God's promise in baptism, "I am with you always, to the end of the age" (Matthew 28:20b) and knows that baptism is a journey with God in life through death to eternal life. Ashes were once used as a cleansing agent in the absence of soap. The ashes as a cleansing agent can be understood as a symbol for the cleansing in baptism. The tradition of the purple season of passionate pondering of the cross, Lent, has a major focus on baptism. The ashes, like the water of baptism, tell us of death and resurrection, of sin and grace, of law and gospel.[3]

This is seen in Psalm 51:1-2, the great confessional Psalm of David:

---

3 Philip H. Pfatteicher and Carlos R. Messerli, *Manual on the Liturgy, Lutheran Book of Worship*, pp. 307-308.

Have mercy on me, O God, according to your steadfast love; according to your abundant mercy blot out my transgressions. Wash me thoroughly from my iniquity, and cleanse me from my sin.

Because the tramp clown lives on the fringes of life, the clown lives very close to nature. This clown knows how ashes are used in nature for cleansing. A forest fire caused by lightning leaves hundreds, maybe thousands of acres of ashes only to turn a bright green with the following months of rain and sunshine. The tramp knows how some farmers may use burning of a field for new growth. The tramp clown sees the cross in the center of creation and sees creation and redemption as one act of God. Through the cross of Christ, the tramp sees that the whole race can die and be raised to new life. Everything that originates in life, everything of God's creation in which there is a blessing now serves the restoration of the new person. This is what happens in baptism.

The great reformer Dr. Martin Luther understood the role of the tramp clown well. For he not only put on the costume of the sackcloth and ashes of the Black Cloister of the Augustinian Order, but took a vow of poverty and lived life on the fringes. Perhaps it was in living life and seeing life much like a tramp clown that gave him such a clear picture of the gospel of baptism as he wrote in the Small Catechism, published in 1529:

WHAT DOES SUCH BAPTIZING WITH WATER SIGNIFY?
ANSWER: It signifies that the old Adam in us, together will all sins and evil lusts, should be drowned by daily sorrow and repentance and be put to death, ant that the new man should come forth daily and rise up, cleansed and righteous, to live forever in God's presence.

WHERE IS THIS WRITTEN?
ANSWER: In Romans 6:4, St. Paul wrote, "We were buried therefore with him by baptism into death, so that as

Christ was raised from the dead by the glory of the
Father, we too might walk in newness of life."[4]

Danish theologian, Regin Prenter, also expresses it well:

In other words, through faith in Christ the individual
becomes the battleground for the struggle between life
and death. And now everything in his life—the spiritual
and the physical, the internal and the external—is
drawn into this struggle. Condemning the old Adam to
death is not only a forensic act of the heavenly court-
room; the old Adam is assailed from all sides here on
earth. Everything which originates in death, everything
which is in league with the powers of destruction now
contributes to the fight against the old Adam; it is
turned into that cross which is laid upon the old Adam
and which he must carry until he is nailed to it in death,
never again to arise.[5]

There is balance as the tramp walks in the dichotomy of
death and resurrection, darkness and light, law and gospel, sin
and grace. It is a baptismal walk, totally immersed in the Christ
event. Throughout this walk the clown raises the question "What
does this mean?" Faith always seeks understanding. Every day
the gospel of baptism strengthens the hope of resurrection no
matter what surrounds the tramp clown. The tramp clown lives in
the shadows of life and ministers to the people living in the shadows. This clown points people of the shadows to the light of the
world, Jesus Christ. In the cross of Christ the tramp clown knows
that God offers hope to the hopeless.

John H. Towsen in his book *Clowns* visualizes this role of
bringing hope to people as he describes Emmett Kelly's character, Weary Willie:

4 The Book of Concord (1580) translated and edited by Theodore G. Tappert
(St. Louis, Mo.: Concordia Publishing House) 1959, p. 349.
5 Regin Prenter, *Creation and Redemption* (Philadelphia: Fortress Press, 1969),
p. 210.

A boy in the audience offers Kelly a peanut. Finding
the shell too hard to crack, he drags over an available
sledgehammer. A single blow and nothing remains
except peanut dust. And this makes him even sadder.
"I am a sad and ragged little guy," explained Kelly in his
autobiography, "who is very serious about everything he
attempts—no matter how futile or foolish it appears to
be. I am the hobo who found out the hard way that the
deck is stacked, the dice "frozen," the race fixed and the
wheel crocked, but there is always present that one, tiny
forlorn spark of hope still glimmering in his soul which
makes him keep on trying."[6]

C. Welton Gaddy also notices how a tramp clown can communicate both pathos and pleasure as he describes what he sees
in the costume, face, and action of Emmett Kelly in his book,
God's Clowns:

Did you ever watch Emmett Kelly, the professional
clown's clown? At first glance Willie—Kelly's circus
name—was a picture of pathos: thin-soled, knottily
laced, worn out, oversized shoes; dark and dirty clothing
that hung awkwardly in layers of wrinkles, tears, and
patches and had frayed edges; baggy, sagging pants; a
bulky, flapping, much too large coat; a sloppy mis-
matched tie clipped smugly to a tarnished shirt by a
rough wooden clothespin; splintery hairs protruding
from underneath a battered old derby.

Willies face was utterly captivating: an orange-red bul-
bous nose; cheeks and chin darkened by face paint,
leaving the impression that he was unshaven or dirty;
lips and mouth whitened in a forlorn expression; eyes
obviously lively but most often downcast, with a con-

6 John H. Towsen, *Clowns* (New York: Hawthorn Books, Inc., 1976), pp. 296-298.
Towsen quotes from pages 125-126 of Emmett Kelly's autobiography *Clown*.

stant hint of tears. By Kelly's own assessment, Willie was a "forlorn and melancholy little hobo." Pathos was the perception at first glance. Yet to see Willie was to experience joy. To watch him perform was to know laughter. The very presence of Emmett Kelly as Willie the clown communicated both pathos and pleasure. His face was mournful but his actions graceful. From others' problems came the incentive for his pranks. From the tears that trickled down his cheeks came the smiles that spread across the faces of his observers.[7]

I had the honor and privilege of learning skills in clowning from Mark Anthony during the last few years of his life. I developed a friendship with Mark through my relationship with Wayne and Marty Scott, who occasionally attended worship services at St. John Lutheran Church in Winter Park, Florida, where I was one of the pastors at that time. They were perhaps Mark's closest friends. They were family and lived together.

Mark was a passionate teacher of clowning. It is what he had done all of his life. He left home in his early teens to join the circus and the circus became his home and family until he died. Mark was a marvelous clown and teacher. His passion was not only for the art of clowning but for the students as well. He is in the first group of six clowns inducted in 1989 into the Clown Hall of Fame, formerly in Delavan, Wisconsin, presently in Milwaukee, Wisconsin. He was a tireless clown in the circus who was known for his pratfalls, energy, creative prop building, and love of peo-

---

7 C. Welton Gaddy, *God's Clowns: Messengers of the Good News* (San Francisco: Harper & Row Publishers, 1990), pp. 72-73.

ple. Some have claimed him the World's Foremost Sculptor of Foam Rubber. There are stories of how he carved a life-size elephant out of foam rubber. Mark truly lived life inside-out.

Mark was not a sad tramp clown. His makeup gave the impression that he lived close to the earth and close to the Creator God. The grease paint of his clown face showed the marks of the earth, of being a clod, of knowing the fallen nature of humanity. Sometimes he even had a fly stuck on his nose, a picture of life. Around his neck, Tony, as his friends called him, wore a dog collar and a bell, a picture of the reality of a materialistic world that pushes and pulls for more and more. To make the audience even more aware of this he painted his tongue hanging out of the right side of his mouth. Aware of the pain and the fallen nature of humanity, Tony was not a sad-face tramp clown. His makeup and character were always signs of hope and love.

Often Tony would have a buzzard on his shoulder or coming out of his hat. It was more than a gag to draw attention to himself. It was another word picture. I asked him to tell me about the buzzard. This man of few words simply and quietly replied, "A buzzard knows that a little is enough!" In a world that cries out for more power, more money, more stuff, the one who is of the earth and with the breath of God knows that a little is enough. He loved very easily and was easily loved.

But as servants of God we have commended ourselves in every way: through great endurance, in afflictions, hardships, calamities, beatings, imprisonments, riots, labors, sleepless nights, hunger; by purity, knowledge patience, kindness, holiness of spirit, genuine love, truthful speech, and the power of God; with the weapons of righteousness for the right hand and for the left; in honor and dishonor, in ill repute and good repute. We are treated as impostors, and yet are true; as unknown, and yet are well known; as dying, and see—we are alive; as punished and yet not killed; as sorrowful, yet

always rejoicing; as poor, yet making many rich; as having nothing, and yet possessing everything.
(2 Corinthians 6:4-10)

Mark Anthony knew what gives life. His eyes were directly connected to his heart. He could communicate so well without words. He was a quiet man who could communicate so loudly and clearly. Even in his last moments of his life he continued to teach me.

Battling cancer, Tony was hospitalized at Florida Hospital very near the congregation I was called to serve as pastor. I went to see him daily. Other members of our clown troupe, The Life In Christ Circus, also visited him regularly. Every day there was another clown in his room with him. He was so well respected and loved. I joined his faithful friends, Wayne and Marty Scott and Leon McBryde in prayer at every visit. He knew his days were few in number. But a little is enough!

On one of my visits a priest from the Roman Catholic Church came to hear his confession and give him last rites. Because Tony had been connected to the Roman Catholic Church as a child and continued to give offerings to the church as he traveled throughout the world with the circus, this was a comforting moment. But because he traveled all his life with the circus, Tony had never been a member of a congregation. Because of some ecclesiastical rule he was told that his funeral could not be in a Roman Catholic congregation. I looked into his eyes as tears welled up and rolled down his cheeks and said to him, "Then we will do the worship service at St. John!"

He smiled at me, squeezed my hand to draw me closer to him, fighting the cancer in his throat, he whispered, "I don't want a clown service!"

"I know. You want a service of resurrection. We will celebrate the resurrected life of Mark Anthony. We will thank God for the love of Jesus Christ. We will tell people of your faith!" I boldly exclaimed.

He never said a word. He just smiled.

And we did celebrate the resurrected life of Mark Anthony with a wonderful memorial service. Clowns and circus people gathered from all over the world. Many people from Ringling Bros. and Barnum & Bailey Circus and Clyde Beaty Cole Brothers Circus came. Other clowns came from national organizations such as Clowns of American, International and World Clown Association, and those from various local clown ministries. This beloved teacher had touched so many of us. We thanked God for the gift of grace in Jesus Christ and for the life of Mark Anthony who created a word picture for us in life and in death. We wept and we laughed. Even in death we all could see Tony's smile. It was the smile of hope, for he was of the earth and close to the Creator God. He lived with the breath of God.

After the memorial service the strange group of people gathered in the fellowship hall to continue celebrating the resurrected life of Mark Anthony. It was like a family reunion. We had a great meal and then sat around and told family stories. We looked at old photo slides of circus days, connected faces with names, and shared stories of a life of faith and fantasy.

Great tramp clowns like Emmett Kelly, Otto Griebling, Mark Anthony, and Jim Howle are needed not only for the Greatest Show On Earth and the Clown Hall of Fame, but for the balance of life. These clowns are great communicators. They create word pictures that guide people through life. Because the tramp clown lives life close to the earth, in the dust, and with those who live on the fringes of life, the style of clowning is very different than that of the whiteface or auguste clown. Instead of working hard to get the audience to laugh, the tramp clown's look of failure and deeds of futility invite the audience to work hard at bringing cheer and laughter to the clown. The tramp or hobo clown keeps us close to the earth, aware of our humanity and aware of our hope in Christ Jesus.

The Whiteface Clown

He is risen! He is risen indeed! [8]

One of the most dramatic transitions in the cycle of the Christian church year is that of moving from the season of Lent to the season of Easter. The purple time of passionate pondering on the cross of Christ, called Lent, is a very quiet time of mediation. People look closely at the cross and whisper, "Shh!" and "Hmm?" However, Easter is filled with bright, joyful colors. People look at the empty tomb of Jesus, the Christ, and shout, "Yes! Wow! He's risen! He's risen indeed! Alleluia!" This transition is best seen in the Easter Vigil. In clown ministry this transition is best seen in the whiteface clown. Many Christians who are not part of congregations that use specific and historical liturgies may not be familiar with the transition of an Easter Vigil. It is rich in symbolism.

Anciently, the Easter Vigil was a watch during the night for signs of a new day, the rising sun. So the worship service was done late on Holy Saturday evening and concluded in the next day. The Easter Vigil is a little less obvious than the worship services of Easter, yet it is filled with signs of hope and the joy of salvation through the death and resurrection of the Christ:

> The climax of the sacred triduum that began on Maundy Thursday is reached in this service which abounds in archetypal imagery that evokes responses from deep within the human psyche: darkness and light, death and life, chaos and order, slavery and freedom. The cross is vindicated as the Lord's throne (already prefigured on Good Friday), and the fullness of salvation finds expression—creation and redemption, old covenant and new covenant, Baptism and Eucharist. Through the word, the sacraments are revealed as symbols of God's salvation of humanity. This most holy night is the solemn memori-

8 Responsive greeting used by pastor and people on the Festival of the Resurrection, Easter.

al of the central mystery of salvation—Christ's saving death and mighty rising.[9]

The Easter Vigil worship may include the Eucharist (Lord's Supper), but many congregations leave this great feast of thanksgiving for the full Festival of the Resurrection on Easter morning. The Easter Vigil has three main parts: Service of Light, Service of Readings, and the Service of Baptism. The paraments in the chancel are changed to bring the message of Easter. The paraments are white or gold in dramatic contrast to the stripped altar on Maundy Thursday and the black veils of Good Friday. All veils are removed. Plants and flowers are brought in to fill the worship space with the colors of spring and new life. An Alleluia banner that was taken down during Lent is again hung high for the people to see. Traditionally, the people do not speak or sing the "Alleluia!" during the season of Lent. But now for the Easter Vigil and Easter season it is shouted with joy. Most Easter hymns are filled with powerful, joyful, and glorious sounds of alleluia.

The first part of this transitional service is the Service of Light. Light is the connecting symbol of creation and redemption. Light symbolizes the Creator God's first work, and light is the symbol of our risen Christ, shining as the rising sun, conquering the darkness of sin and death. Note the following parallels in the Old Testament passage of Genesis 1 and the prologue of John 1. Then note the proclamation of Jesus in John 8 below:

> In the beginning when God crated the heavens and the earth, the earth was a formless void and darkness covered the face of the deep, while a wind from God swept over the face of the waters. Then God said, "Let there be light;" and there was light. And God saw that the light was good; and God separated the light from the darkness. God called the light Day, and the darkness he

9 Philip H. Pfatteicher and Carlos R. Messerli, *Manual on the Liturgy, Lutheran Book of Worship*, p. 326.

called Night. And there was evening and there was morning, the first day. *(Genesis 1:1-5)*

In the beginning was the Word, and the Word was with God, and the Word was God. He was in the beginning with God. All things came into being through him, and without him not one thing came into being. What has come into being in him was the life, and the life was the light of all people. The light shines in the darkness, and the darkness did not overcome it. *(John 1:1-5)*

Again Jesus spoke to them, saying, "I am the light of the world. Whoever follows me will never walk in darkness but will have the light of life." *(John 8:12)*

To visualize, or bring to light, the connection of creation and redemption, the people gather in another room of the church building rather than the nave and chancel. Each person is given a candle or they are asked to bring their baptismal candle from home. This room is kept as dark as one can safely do in a public gathering. I usually suggest that children too young to hold a candle responsively and safely be given glow sticks instead of lighting their candles. The assisting minister, who carries the paschal candle, symbolizing Christ, the light of the world, lights the paschal candle. The presiding minister says, "May the light of Christ, rising in glory, dispel the darkness of our hearts and minds."[10]

Much like a clown in ministry, the Easter Vigil paints a picture connecting Old Testament promise and New Testament fulfillment in Jesus Christ. The people process into the nave and chancel of the church, following the light of the paschal candle, just as the children of Israel were led by a pillar of fire from slavery into freedom of the promise land. Once inside, the people light their candles from the paschal candle. They sing hymns pro-

---

10 Philip H, Pfatteicher and Carlos R. Messerli, *Manual on the Liturgy, Lutheran Book of Worship*, p. 328.

claiming the glory of Jesus, the light of the world. The songs also recall significant biblical people or events—Adam, the Passover, the Exodus, and the Resurrection.

The second part of the Easter Vigil is filled with up to twelve readings from Holy Scripture. The traditions of various denominations will use different number of readings. These readings make the transition from an emphasis on creation to that of Holy Baptism. In all liturgical traditions the first lesson read is always the story of creation. The story of the Exodus is another lesson that is always read.

Because many Christian clowns are not familiar with the symbolism of the Easter Vigil, or my concept of the whiteface clown as the Easter Vigil, I will include all twelve of the Bible readings that are suggested for use during an Easter Vigil. These passages may be very helpful to a whiteface clown as she or he develops character, makeup, costume, and routines:

1. Genesis 1:1—2: 2 tells of creation.
2. Genesis 7:1-5, 11-18; 8:6-18; 9:8-13 tell of the great flood, a foreshadowing of Baptism.
3. Genesis 22:1-8 tells of Abraham's sacrifice of Isaac, a symbol of the sacrifice of the Son of God.
4. Exodus 14:10—15:1 is the crossing of the Red Sea of Israel and a foreshadowing of the deliverance in Baptism.
5. Isaiah 55:1-11 tells of salvation offered to everyone and connects other biblical themes—water, Eucharist, everlasting covenant, conversion, and the word of creation.
6. Baruch 3:9-37, from the extra canonical writings[11], is a message of hope to a conquered people.

---

11 Barauch is one of the deuterocanonical books. You will find it in Bibles of the Catholic tradition. It is not found in the Hebrew Bible, but in the Greek Old Testament, the Septuagint, it is placed between Jeremiah and Lamentations. In the Vulgate it is placed immediately following Lamentations. According to its introduction in 1:1-14, it was written in Babylon by Baruch after the deportation and sent to Jerusalem to be read at liturgical gatherings. The writing of Baruch gives information about the Jewish communities in the Dispersion and the ways in which their religious life was sustained.

7. Ezekiel 37:1-14 tells of the valley of dry bones and their being brought to life as an obvious picture of the resurrection.

8. Isaiah 4:2-6 tells of God washing and cleansing the people.

9. Exodus 12:1-14 tells of the institution of the meal of remembrance, the Passover, that Jesus uses to institute the Lord's Supper, the Eucharist.

10. Jonah 3:1-10 tells of the conversion of Ninevah from Jonah's preaching and points to baptismal repentance.

11. Deuteronomy 31:19-30 is a stern warning of Moses to the people of God to live in the covenant of God. This lesson is the last of the four in the Roman Catholic rite of the Easter Vigil. The song of Moses is sung following this reading, celebrating the faithfulness of God.

12. Daniel 3:1-29 tells the story of the three men who were thrown into the fire because of their steadfast faith.[12]

After the last lesson is read, the song of the three young men who were thrown into the furnace is sung usually by the choir. This canticle has a Latin name: Benedicite, Omnia Opera. Again, because so few people may be familiar with it and because it provides wonderful insights to the character, makeup, costume, and routines of a whiteface clown, I will print it in this book.

All you works of the Lord, bless the Lord—
Praise him and magnify him forever.
You angels of the Lord, bless the Lord;
You heavens, bless the Lord;
All you powers of the Lord, bless the Lord—
Praise him and magnify him forever.
You sun and moon, bless the Lord;
You stars of heaven, bless the Lord;
You showers and dew, bless the Lord—
Praise him and magnify him forever.

12 Twelve of these lessons with further description are found in *Manual on the Liturgy, Lutheran Book of Worship*, pp. 331-333.

You winds of God, bless the Lord;
  You fire and heat bless the Lord;
You winter and summer, bless the Lord—
  Praise him and magnify him forever.
You dews and frost, bless the Lord;
  You frost and cold, bless the Lord;
You ice and snow, bless the Lord—
  Praise him and magnify him forever.
You nights and days, bless the Lord;
  You light and darkness, bless the Lord;
You lightnings and clouds, bless the Lord—
  Praise him and magnify him forever.
Let the earth bless the Lord;
  You mountains and hills, bless the Lord;
All you green things that grow on the earth, bless the Lord—
  Praise him and magnify him forever.
You wells and springs, bless the Lord;
  You rivers and seas, bless the Lord;
You whales and all who move in the waters, bless the Lord—
  Praise him and magnify him forever.
All you birds of the air, bless the Lord;
  All you beasts and cattle, bless the Lord;
All you children of mortals, bless the Lord—
  Praise him and magnify him forever.
You people of God, bless the Lord;
  You priests of the Lord, bless the Lord;
You servants of the Lord, bless the Lord—
  Praise him and magnify him forever.
You spirits and souls of the righteous, bless the Lord;
  You pure and humble of heart, bless the Lord;
Let us bless the Father and the Son and the Holy Spirit—
  Praise him and magnify him forever.[13]

The liturgy of the Easter Vigil moves from the Service of

13 *Lutheran Book of Worship, Ministers Desk Edition* (Minneapolis: Augsburg Publishing House, 1978), pp. 151-152.

Light to the Service of Readings and next to the Service of
Baptism. Again, this service connects creation and redemption. In
the early Christian church many believers and their families were
baptized during the season celebrating Easter and especially during the Easter Vigil. Many theologians describe the letter of
1 Peter as a baptismal liturgy used by the early Christians.[14] In a
previous chapter I had already established the connection of creation and redemption in the sacrament of Baptism. The imagery
of the Easter Vigil visualizes that connection as the candidates for
baptism now surround the baptismal font.

> The font is the womb of the church. As the Spirit once
> moved upon the Virgin Mary so that she conceived and
> bore the Son of God, so now we ask that in this font the
> church may bear new children of God.[15]

The words of the baptismal liturgy and the actions of the pastor continue to connect creation and redemption. The pastor says
a thanksgiving prayer for the gift of water and parts the water
with the sign of the cross when saying the words, "baptizing
them in the name of the Father, and of the Son, and of the Holy
Spirit." The pastor may blow over the water after saying the
words, "Pour out your Holy Spirit," thus symbolizing the Wind,
Power, or Spirit of the God of creation. In this thanksgiving
prayer when the pastor asks God to wash away sins and cleanse
those being baptized, some pastors dip the bottom of the paschal
candle into the water of the baptismal font. Baptism is a total
immersion into the Christ event. Christ was immersed into death
and was raised to new life. Those who are baptized are dead to
sin, but raised to walk in the newness of life.

What follows the prayer of thanksgiving for water is the
renunciation of the devil, the works of the devil, and all evil
ways. Then comes the profession of faith, usually the Apostles'

14 G.R. Beasley-Murray, *Baptism in the New Testament* (London: MacMillian &
Co. Ltd., 1963), pp. 254-255.

15 Philip H. Pfatteicher and Carolos R. Messerli, *Manual on the Liturgy, Lutheran
Book of Worship*, p. 333.

Creed. To affirm all those who have been baptized, during the creed, the pastor may take an evergreen branch, symbolizing eternal life, dip it into the water in the baptismal font, and sprinkle the heads of the people assembled.

After the baptisms, if there is no Eucharist (Lord's Supper) within the Easter Vigil, then the worship service concludes with the people leaving the church with joy, but in silence, to return to their homes. They are prepared to return to the church later that morning for the celebration of the Feast of the Resurrection. There they will shout their alleluias!

The imagery for the whiteface clown continues to build in the celebration of Easter. Of all the Sundays and other celebrations of the Christian Church, Easter is the feast day that is attended by the most people. Those who plan worship on Easter Sunday pull out all the stops. The nave is splashed with the colors of new life in banners and flowers. Some use the sound of the birds of spring. Brass, woodwinds, and string ensembles proclaim the joy of resurrection. The timpani pound like hearts full of life. Like heavenly angels, the choirs, made up of the voices of children of all ages, sing of the glory of God. As a sign of new life, many of the people come dressed in new clothes of bright colors. The people join their hearts and voices in the songs of Easter. They move their bodies in the dance of Easter. They shout together in the liturgy, "He's risen indeed!"

In Christian clowning the whiteface clown is the clown whose character, makeup, costume, and actions create a bridge between Good Friday and Easter. The whiteface clown is the Easter Vigil. This wonderful clown, filled with the images of Easter, paints a picture of the empty cross and the empty tomb. The cross and tomb are empty, but our lives are full—full of joy, color, faith, hope, and love. The Easter clown paints pictures of the presence of this foolish and gracious God who simply and powerfully loves people. This clown constantly shows a love that can only come from God, a love with no strings. The whiteface clown is truly graceful, and grace-filled.

My good friend, Penne Sewall, who is a marvelous Christian and whiteface clown, describes this type of clown as the joy-bringer and a vulnerable lover.

> In clown ministry, this clown is called the Joy Bringer because the White Face personifies exaggerations of childlikeness as the clown uses symbols such as bubbles or balloons. This clown is a vulnerable and unconditional lover, risk-taker, truster, and creator of ideas. This type is often mischievous and would be the one to tie two clown shoes together. Although the White Face is the
>
>
>
> most carefree of the clown types, the capability to express the tears and sad emotions characteristic of a child is also there. Makeup is an all-white face with simple lines for the features. Primarily black and red colors are used, but other colors such as blue often are added. The White Face usually wears a one-piece jumpsuit or two-piece outfit that coordinates to create a jumper effect.[16]

The Easter Vigil clown, the whiteface, assures us that we have been washed and cleansed in our baptism and born anew as children of this foolish God. This clown reminds us of the joy of our salvation. The whiteface clown brings the hopeful message of Easter to the world.

> See what love the Father has given us, that we should be called children of God; and that is what we are. The reason the world does not know us is that it did not

16 Floyd Shaffer and Penne Sewall, *Clown Ministry*, (Loveland, Colo.: Group Books, 1984), p. 30.

know him. Beloved, we are God's children now; what
we will be has not yet been revealed. What we do know
is this: when he is revealed, we will be like him, for we
will see him as he is. And all who have this hope in him
purify themselves, just as he is pure. *(1 John 3:1-3)*

In one of my earlier books on learning the art of clown ministry, *Welcome to the Sawdust Circle Part II*, I described the
whiteface clown as a creative and open lover of life and people.
This clown takes great risks, has tremendous trust, and is very
clever. Freely the whiteface moves from one emotion to another
and always exposes the heart. The whiteface seems so carefree
because of the boldness of living in faith and joy and loving to
give it away. The whiteface is also called an elegant, elite, or neat
clown. Those words describe the makeup, costume, and character of the whiteface. The whiteface has a beautiful clown face and
invites people to take a closer look at life through his or her character. The closer one gets, the more beauty is seen. Like the
pounding of the timpani during the celebration of Easter, this
clown has a heartthrob for people.[17]

The whiteface clown as we know the clown today has its
beginning in the late 18th century. The great English pantomime
and comic genius, Joseph Grimaldi (1778–1837), is claimed to
be the clown who added the color to the white covering his entire
face.

Grimaldi painted his face white, as did the French
Pierrot, but he also added substantial color to the
mouth, cheeks, and eyebrows. Most pronounced were
the cheeks, which were bedecked with large red trian-
gles, giving his face a far wilder expression than that of
the *enfariné* (flour-covered) Pierrot.[18]

17 Dick Hardel, *Welcome to the Sawdust Circle Part II, Learning the Art of Clown
Ministry* (Orlando, Fla., 1988), pp. 44-45.
18 John Towsen, *Clowns* (New York: Hawthorn Books, Inc, 1976), p. 153.

The circus clowns received their most enduring nickname, "Joey," from Joseph Grimaldi.

In clowning today and in the circus there are two types of whiteface clowns: elegant (neat) and grotesque. Both types of whiteface clowns wear costumes that the colors and pattern are coordinated. The elegant whiteface has a full white face with modest, traditional clown colors of black, red, and, perhaps, a soft blue. This clown wears a white skull cap so that no hair shows and usually a very small but beautiful hat. Glen "Frosty" Little, 1991 Clown Hall of Fame inductee, is a very good example of a traditional elegant whiteface clown.

The grotesque whiteface has bold markings on the white face much like an auguste clown. This clown may exaggerate facial features and costume as well. Often the grotesque white-face clown will wear a colorful wig or show sprouting hair. This clown may also have a definite, funny nose. Felix Adler, 1989 Clown Hall of Fame inductee, is a good example of a grotesque whiteface clown.

In Christian clown ministry, both types of whiteface clowns are Easter Vigil clowns. They both bring resurrection joy to people.

The Easter Vigil clown, the whiteface clown, is not dependent on words. This clown puts the message of Easter joy into action. The face is the first tool of communication for the white-face as for all clowns. The second tool is her or his body. Many Christian clowns choose not to talk. Floyd Shaffer, also a present-day, great whiteface clown, has said that is because Christian worship services have become so dependent on the verbal use of words, that it often more powerful to use mime and pantomime. He gets this concept from the following passage of Scripture:

Little children, let us love, not in word or speech, but in truth and action. *(1 John 3:18)*

In the section entitled "The Non-Verbal Talker" in their book, *Clown Ministry*, Penne Sewall and Floyd Shaffer give more reasons why a clown, especially an Easter clown might choose not to speak:

> In our verbal society it is easy to tell someone, "I care about you," or "I want to help you." Showing this in behavior is another matter. In clown ministry, the non-verbal clown is the WORD becoming ACTION. The clown must show meanings rather than try to explain them. This is a real challenge for clowns, because they must carefully plan how they will convey their message. The people in the audience must listen with their eyes to hear what is being said.[19]

Even for the great Joseph Grimaldi, communicating with one's face and body was more important and powerful than using words.

> Grimaldi had little use for words. His expression was in his face and body. Even his nose, according to another pantomime buff, was a vivacious excrescence capable of exhibiting disdain, fear, anger, even joy.... Speech would have been thrown away in his performance of Clown: every limb of him had a language.[20]

The Easter Vigil clown, the whiteface, moves gracefully among people and brings joy to the fallen human race by connecting creation with redemption. The focus, again, of the Christian whiteface clown is the empty cross and the empty tomb. Splashed with the colors of new life on costume and face, the whiteface points to the resurrected Christ and invites the whole world to join and dance in the Easter parade. The Easter Vigil clown reminds us that Christ is the light of the world and through baptism we have become children of the Light, splashed with the grace of God. The Easter parade is a celebration of the

19 Floyd Shaffer and Penne Sewall, *Clown Ministry*, p. 25.
20 John Towsen, *Clowns* (New York: Hawthorn Books, Inc. 1976), p. 156.

"Yes!" to all of God's promises. The whiteface clown invites the people with love to celebrate the resurrection of Jesus, the Christ by shouting, "Amen!"

> For the Son of God, Jesus Christ, whom we proclaimed among you, Silvanus and Timothy and I, was not "Yes and No;" but in him it is always "Yes." For in him every one of God's promises is a "Yes." For this reason it is through him that we say the "Amen," to the glory of God. But it is God who establishes us with you in Christ and has anointed us, by putting his seal on us and giving us his Spirit in our hearts as a first installment.
> (2 Corinthians 1:19-22)

The Easter Vigil clown reminds us that once we were dead to God in our sins. But God has paid the penalty through the death and resurrection of Jesus Christ. When we were baptized we were immersed into Christ's death on the cross. The clown challenges the baptized to live their baptism daily. Baptism is not a nicely framed certificate, it is a way of life. The clown challenges the people to live as the Easter people of God, filled with the Spirit and sharing the gifts of the Spirit. Immersed in the baptismal faith, the Easter Vigil clown knows the difference between living in slavery of sin and being freed by Christ to serve God. The clown paints a picture of Christ. It is a picture of a bridge made from the wood of the cross. The cross is the bridge that leads to freedom.

> Live by the Spirit, I say, and do not gratify the desires of the flesh. For what the flesh desires is opposed to the Spirit, and what the Spirit desires is opposed to the flesh; for these are opposed to each other, to prevent you from doing what you want. But if you are led by the Spirit, you are not subject to the law. Now the works of the flesh are obvious: fornication, impurity, licentiousness, idolatry, sorcery, enmities, strife, jealousy, anger,

quarrels, dissensions, factions, envy, drunkenness, carous-
ing, and things like these. I am warning you, as I warned
you before; those who do such things will not inherit the
kingdom of God. By contrast, the fruit of the Spirit is
love, joy, peace, patience, kindness, generosity, faithfulness, gentleness, and self-control. There is no law against
such things. And those who belong to Christ Jesus have
crucified the flesh with its passions and desires. If we
live by the Spirit, let us also be guided by the Spirit. Let
us not become conceited, competing against one another, envying one another. *(Galatians 5:16-26)*

The boss clown of the Florida Unit of the
Life in Christ Circus is a wonderful whiteface
clown named Pink E. The *E* stands for Easter.
She stands because of Easter. The exaggerated lines and symbols on her face make her a
grotesque whiteface. She has a larger-than-
life smile on her lips. Neat greasepaint lines
extend from the ends of her smile and connect to a beautiful, glittered red heart on the
crest of each of her cheeks. Her costumes
are always of Easter colors of pink, yellow,
white, or soft blue. She wears a pink wig.
Her face and her costume are all signs of the
joy of Easter. The fruits of the Spirit of Galatians 5 describes her
character—love, joy, peace, patience, kindness, generosity, faithfulness, gentleness, and self-control. These characteristics are
seen in everything she does, whether she is in make up or not.
Pink E lives her life inside-out!

Within the various traditions of the Easter celebrations of the
Christian church, especially the Easter Vigil, the whiteface clown
will find hundreds and perhaps thousands of ideas to touch the
hearts of people with the love of Christ.

The Auguste Clown

We have observed his star at its rising,
And have come to pay him homage. (Matthew 2:2)

The central theme of Christian theology is highlighted in the seasons of Lent and Easter. This is a theology of the cross. The seasons of Christmas and Epiphany prepare us for Lent and Easter. The birth narratives of Jesus, the Christ, and the coming of the magi raise the first question of Christology: "Who is this Jesus?" The Christmas stories give us an even bigger picture of the foolishness of God in the incarnation, which we have already covered in this book. It just doesn't make sense for the Omnipotent, Omnipresent, and All Glorious, Creator God to appear in such common and hidden ways. Why would the Creator God choose to reveal the nature of God by Jesus being born in stable-cave and in a manger for a bed? Why would God choose to surround this newborn king with lowly shepherds? The Babe of Bethlehem is revealed as God and the splendor of the divine glory bursts through humanity.

Epiphany is the season of the church year that is like a bridge, connecting Christmas and Easter. The word *Epiphany* comes from two Greek words, *epi* and *phainein*, meaning "to shine forth."[21] The glory of God shines forth in the birth and ministry of Jesus Christ. The season of Epiphany gives a wonderful description of an auguste clown. Much like an Irish folklore of the leprechaun searching for the pot of gold at the end of a rainbow, the auguste clown follows the light in search for the source of the glory of God.

Christmas proclaims the incarnation, that God became a human being in Jesus. It is a celebration of a historical event. Epiphany is not a celebration of an event, but rather presents an idea that is only seen in the life of Jesus. The idea is that this his-

---

21 *Webster's New Collegiate Dictionary* (Springfield, Mass.: G. & C. Merriam Co., Publishers, 1958), p. 277. Also see F. Wilbur Gingrich and Frederick W. Danker, *Shorter Lexicon of the Greek New Testament* (Chicago: University of Chicago Press, 1983), pp. 72-73 and 209.

torical Jesus, born in a manger in Bethlehem, is God. The emphasis of this season is that the world can now see Jesus as God.

> And with Word became flesh and lived among us, and
> we have seen his glory, the glory as of a father's only
> son, full of grace and truth. *(John 1:14)*

In the birth of Jesus, God enters a world turned upside-down
through sin. Sin caused a separation between the creator and creation and between relationship of human beings to the rest of creation. It is described in God's curse in Genesis 3. In an upside-
down world the glory of God becomes hidden.

> The Lord God said to the serpent, "Because you have
> done this, cursed are you among all animals and among
> all wild creatures; upon your belly you shall go, and dust
> you shall eat all the days of your life. I will put enmity
> between you and the woman, and between your off-
> spring and hers; he will strike you head, and you will
> strike his heel." To the woman he said, "I will greatly
> increase your pangs in childbearing; in pain you shall
> bring forth children, yet your desire shall be for your
> husband, and he shall rule over you." And to the man
> he said, "Because you have listened to the voice of your
> wife, and have eaten of the tree about which I com-
> manded you, 'You shall not eat of it,' cursed is the
> ground because of you; in toil you shall eat of it all the
> days of your life; thorns and thistles it shall bring forth
> for you; and you shall eat the plants of the field. By the
> sweat of your face you shall eat bread until you return
> to the ground, for out of it you were taken; you are dust
> and to dust you shall return." *(Genesis 3:14-19)*

Through Jesus Christ, God's foolish plan to redeem human
beings and give them the opportunity to walk upright in an
upside-down world was revealed. Epiphany brings light to darkness. It focuses upon an upside-down world through the light of

Jesus. Through the light of Jesus Christ all of creation is changed. The focus of Epiphany is much like the work of a photographer. The lens of a camera, much like the human eye, sees everything upside-down. When the photo is developed the picture is turned right-side-up. The human brain does a similar job. The brain inverts the image brought by the optic nerve through the retina of the eye. Dr. Paul Bretscher writes about this imagery in a wonderful little book, *The World: Upside Down or Right Side Up?*

> The upside-downness of the world is its ruin. Speaking theologically again, we would call it the alienation of the world from God. God wants to be at one with the world, but He will not tolerate or conform to its upside-down character or let us make Him what we are. He is determined rather to turn us right side up.

> That is where the Gospel comes into the story. God sent his Son Jesus into the upside-down world, and Jesus walked in it right side up. The people who had to live with him found this intolerable, and when they could not get Him to walk upside down the way they did, they finally had to kill Him. But some did believe in Him, and thereby were turned right side up, walking as He walked. These included the apostles, who went out and preached that Jesus had risen from the dead, that He whom the world had condemned as upside down was right side up after all, and that it was the world which hated Jesus that was really upside down. People did not find this kind of preaching easy to take either. In Thessalonica they even complained, "These men who have turned the world upside down have come here also!" (Acts 17: 6). They wanted no other world than the one they had, and would not believe that what the apostles were really doing was turning the world right side up.[22]

22 Paul G. Bretscher, *The World Upside Down or Right Side Up?* (St. Louis, Mo.: Concordia Publishing House, 1964), pp. 2-3.

In Jesus, the Christ, God turns the religious view of the Jews upside-down by revealing that this same God is God for all people, Gentiles as well as Jews. Epiphany is the Gentile feast of faith. This festival of Epiphany also called the Twelfth Day, the Feast of the Three Kings, or the Manifestation of God.[23] The scripture lessons for Epiphany show God's foolish plan of turning an upside-down world right-side-up through Christ.

The Old Testament shows Yahweh as a God of signs and wonders. Through these signs and wonders Yahweh is seen in two different ways: on one hand God is awesome and far above and beyond the space and time of human beings; and on the other hand, God is intimate and makes his personal presence known. The giving of the law and the Ark of the Covenant, the tabernacle, face of Yahweh, the angel of Yahweh, the glory of Yahweh seen in priestly circles, and even the very name of Yahweh are signs of a close relationship with God. But smoke, thunder, earthquakes, wind, storms, fire, etc., are all signs of the awesome, holy God, above and beyond human beings and unapproachable.[24]

Epiphany is a revelation of the same two natures of Jesus, the Christ. He is true man and also truly God. The Christian church today continues to faithfully confess the two natures of Jesus' humanity and divinity in with words of the Nicene Creed.

We believe in one Lord, Jesus Christ, the only Son of God, eternally begotten of the Father, God from God, Light from Light, true God from true God, begotten, not made, of one Being with the Father. Through him all things were made. For us and for our salvation he came down from heaven; by the power of the Holy Spirit he became incarnate from the virgin Mary, and was made man. For our sake he was crucified under Pontius Pilate; he suffered death and was buried. On the third day he

---

23 Fred H. Lindemann, The Sermon and the Propers, (St. Louis, Mo.: Concordia Publishing House, 1966), Vol. 1, p. 141.

24 George A. Buttrick, editor, *The Interpreter's Dictionary of the Bible* (Nashville, Tenn.: Abingdon Press, 1962), Vol. 2, pp. 417-430.

rose again in accordance with the Scriptures; he ascended into heaven and is seated at the right hand of the Father. He will come again in glory to judge the living and the dead, and his kingdom will have no end.[25]

Epiphany steadily develops the vision of the glory of God seen in the life of Jesus from the lessons of the festival of Epiphany to the lessons of the following Sundays in Epiphany. From the coming of the magi, through his miracles, to the transfiguration, the glory of God shines forth in Jesus, the Christ. Simeon saw the glory of God revealed in the child, Jesus, when he held the baby in the temple:

Master, now you are dismissing your servant in peace, according to your word; for my eyes have seen your salvation, which you have prepared in the presence of all peoples, a light for revelation to the Gentiles and for glory to your people Israel. *(Luke 2:29-32)*

Just as the tramp clown can learn about his or her character from studying the lessons for Ash Wednesday and Lent; and the whiteface clown can learn from the lessons of the Easter Vigil; so also the auguste clown can learn much by taking a close look at the scripture lessons for Epiphany.

The psalmody for the festival of Epiphany is Psalm 72:1-7, 10-14. The psalm stresses how the Messiah will turn an upside-down world right-side-up. It also says that many nations will fall down before this king.

There is a focus on missions in the first lesson as the prophet Isaiah gives us a vision of the messianic kingdom. In the darkness of an upside-down world, the city of God is glowing with light because the King has come. Gentiles come to the light:

25 *Lutheran Book of Worship*, (Minneapolis: Augsburg Publishing House, 1978), p. 64.

Arise, shine; for your light has come, and the glory of
the Lord has risen upon you. For darkness shall cover
the earth, and thick darkness the peoples; but the Lord
will arise upon you, and his glory will appear over you.
Nations shall come to your light, and kings to the
brightness of your dawn. Lift up your eyes and look
around; they all gather together, they come to you; your
sons shall come from far away, and your daughters shall
be carried on their nurses' arms. Then you shall see and
be radiant; your heart shall thrill and rejoice, because
the abundance of the sea shall be brought to you, the
wealth of the nations shall come to you. A multitude of
camels shall cover you, the young camels of Midian and
Ephah; all those from Sheba shall come. They shall bring
gold and frankincense, and shall proclaim the praise of
the Lord. *(Isaiah 60:1-6)*

The second lesson stresses how God revealed a mystery of
grace through the foolish plan seen in the Christ event. This foolish plan of salvation is for all nations of people:

This is the reason that I Paul am a prisoner for Christ
Jesus for the sake of you Gentiles—for surely you have
already heard of the commission of God's grace that
was given me for you, and how the mystery was made
known to me by revelation, as I wrote above in a few
words, a reading of which will enable you to perceive
my understanding of the mystery of Christ. In former
generations this mystery was not made known to
humankind, as it has now been revealed to his holy
apostles and prophets by the Spirit: that is, the Gentiles
have become fellow heirs, members of the same body,
and sharers in the promise in Christ Jesus through the
gospel. Of this gospel I have become a servant according to the gift of God's grace that was given me by the

working of his power. Although I am the very least of all the saints, this grace was given to me to bring to the Gentiles the news of the boundless riches of Christ, and to make everyone see what is the plan of the mystery hidden for ages in God who created all things; so that through the church the wisdom of God in its rich variety might now be made known to the rulers and authorities in heavenly places. This was in accordance with the eternal purpose that he has carried out in Christ Jesus our Lord, in whom we have access to God in boldness and confidence through faith in him. (Ephesians 3:1-12)

The gospel lesson for Epiphany shows that the expectant Israel knew who the new king was that the magi were searching for and knew where to find him, but they did not go. There was no light of the glory of God for them. On the other hand, the Gentiles followed the star and in Jesus saw the glory of God. They worshipped him.

In the time of King Herod, after Jesus was born in Bethlehem of Judea, wise men from the East came to Jerusalem, asking, "Where is the child who has been born king of the Jews? For we observed his star at its rising, and have come to pay him homage." When King Herod heard this, he was frightened, and all Jerusalem with him; and calling together all the chief priests and scribes of the people, he inquired of them where the Messiah was to be born. They told him, "In Bethlehem of Judea; for so it has been written by the prophet:

'And you, Bethlehem, in the land of Judah, are by no means least among the rulers of Judah; for from you shall come a ruler who is to shepherd my people Israel.'"

Then Herod secretly called for the wise men and learned from them the exact time when the star had appeared. Then he sent them to Bethlehem, saying, "Go and search diligently for the child; and when you have found him, bring me word so that I may also go and pay him homage." When they had heard the king, they set out; and there, ahead of them, went the star that they had seen in its rising, until it stopped over the place where the child was. When they saw that the star had stopped, they were overwhelmed with joy. On entering the house, they saw the child with Mary his mother; and they knelt down and paid him homage. Then, opening their treasure chests, they offered him gifts of gold, frankincense, and myrrh. And having been warned in a dream not to return to Herod, they left for their own country by another road. *(Matthew 2:1-12)*

The scripture lessons for the Sundays in Epiphany continue to show the glory of God in the life of Jesus, the Messiah. The lessons keep raising the Christological question, "Who is this Jesus?" Who is this Jesus who can carry on a theological discussion with the religious teachers in the synagogue? Who is this Jesus who can turn water into wine? Who is this Jesus who in the sermon on the mountain changes the law? Who is this Jesus on whom the Holy Spirit descended and remained? Who is this Jesus, that the devil would tempt him with a plan that made sense? Who is this Jesus who fulfills the prophecy of Isaiah? Who is this Jesus who fills a boat with fish, heals the leper, has authority over wind and wave, makes the lame to walk, the blind to see, and cast out demons?

The gospel lesson for the last Sunday in Epiphany is the transfiguration story. In fact, this Sunday is often called Transfiguration Sunday. After seeing Jesus transfigured, Peter thought it would be a wonderful idea to pitch tents and set up camp on the mountain of glory. That made sense to him. But when Jesus talked of the suffering to come and the glory beyond the suffering, Peter was puzzled. The way of the cross was foolish, but to stay in the safe place of glory made sense to Peter.

With the vision of the glory of God in Jesus, the Christ, who fulfilled the Law and the Prophets, the people of God now move into the season of Lent:

> Six days later, Jesus took with him Peter and James and John, and led them up a high mountain apart, by themselves. And he was transfigured before them, and his clothes became dazzling white, such as no one on earth could bleach them. And there appeared to them Elijah with Moses, who were talking with Jesus. Then Peter said to Jesus, "Rabbi, it is good for us to be here; let us make three dwellings, one for you, one for Moses, and one for Elijah." He did not know what to say, for they were terrified. Then a cloud overshadowed them and from the cloud there came a voice, "This is my Son, the Beloved; listen to him!" Suddenly when they looked around, they saw no one with them any more, but only Jesus. As they were coming down the mountain, he ordered them to tell no one about what they had seen until after the Son of Man had risen from the dead. So they kept the matter to themselves, questioning what this rising from the dead could mean. Then they asked him, "Why do the scribes say that Elijah must come first?" he said to them, "Elijah is indeed coming first to restore all things. How then is it written about the Son of Man, that he is to go through many sufferings and be treated with contempt? But I tell you that Elijah has come, and they did to him what ever they pleased, as it is written about him." *(Mark 9:2-13)*
>
> *(Also compare Luke 9:28-36; Matthew 17:1-9)*

The color of the church paraments changes during the season of Epiphany from white to green and then back to white. On the festival of Epiphany the paraments are white or perhaps even gold, symbolizing the shining light of the glory of God. The gold

also symbolizes the kingly divinity of Jesus shown in the gifts of
the magi. White is also color on Transfiguration Sunday. From
the second Sunday after Epiphany the color is changed to green,
symbolizing a time of spiritual growth and maturation of faith.
As vision of the glory of God seen in Jesus grows, so the ministry and the mission of the people of God grows.[26]

Epiphany is the season of beholding the glory of God made
manifest in the life of Christ. It is looking at an upside-down
world turned right-side-up through the presence of the glory of
God in Jesus. In the season of Epiphany the people of God discover the glory of God in the midst of their lives by looking from
every angle of the life of Jesus. Epiphany is a time of beholding,
wondering, discovering, and moving from the safe places into the
needed areas of ministry.

The auguste clown is the Epiphany clown, creating a bridge
from Christmas to Easter. The auguste clown creates the bridge
with the wood from the Christmas manger. The Epiphany clown
beholds the world from every angle of the life of Jesus Christ.
The Epiphany clown is always searching for a ray of glory, is full
of wonder, and often puzzled.

Historically the auguste clown was first seen in the circus in
the 19th century. There was a need for a simpleton, a country
bumpkin clown who could be the butt end of the jokes and
pranks of the whiteface clown. That type of comedy was seen in
the United States in the 21st century in the likes of Laurel and
Hardy, Abbott and Costello, or George Burns and Gracie Allen.
The auguste clown rarely understands or sees the whole picture,
but is certain that the little portion of the picture he or she does
have is enough. This clown can be extremely busy while doing
nothing.

The word *auguste* is derived from the Berlin dialect of 19th-
century German. Tom Belling, the son of an American circus
owner, was perhaps the first auguste clown. Belling traveled

26 Philip H. Pfatteicher and Carlos R. Messerli, *Manual on the Liturgy, Lutheran
Book of Worship*, p. 20.

through Europe and Russia with the circus as an equestrian and acrobat. In 1869, while performing with the Renz's Circus in Berlin, he was dared to go out and show himself as he had shown himself to his friends. He had put his wig on backwards, twisted the curls and tied them in a knot that stood straight up at the back of his head. As he was entering the circus ring, he had a collision with Renz, the circus director. To the surprise of Belling, Renz loved the new clown look. Belling tripped several times trying to leave the circus and people laughed loudly and shouted, "Auguste!" which means "stupid" in the Berlin dialect. The auguste look and character of Belling was so well loved by the audience and Renz that he received a new contract.[27]

The auguste clown exaggerates many events of the human

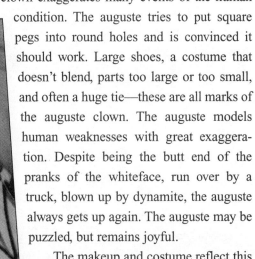

condition. The auguste tries to put square pegs into round holes and is convinced it should work. Large shoes, a costume that doesn't blend, parts too large or too small, and often a huge tie—these are all marks of the auguste clown. The auguste models human weaknesses with great exaggeration. Despite being the butt end of the pranks of the whiteface, run over by a truck, blown up by dynamite, the auguste always gets up again. The auguste may be puzzled, but remains joyful.

The makeup and costume reflect this puzzled, clumsy, and klutzy character. The background of the face is flesh tone.

Exaggerated eyes of white grease paint, usually lined with black, are the main features of the auguste. The auguste clown is always searching, always trying to figure out the logic of an event or idea. The eyes are like windows from which the auguste looks at life. The second important feature of an

27 John H. Towsen, *Clowns* (New York: Hawthorn Books, Inc., 1976), pp. 206-209; 371.

auguste's clown face is the mouth. The mouth, too, is white grease paint lined with red or black.[28]

Perhaps the most recognized auguste clown face in the American circus is that of Lou Jacobs. He was the most photographed clown in America and the only clown to appear on a five-cent American stamp issued in 1966 while he was still living. He was inducted into the Clown Hall of Fame with the first group of six in 1989. One of the features of Lou's clown face included an extended pointed head that made him very unique. The audience laughed and laughed at this outstanding clown who was often outwitted by his own dog.

Two other well-known auguste circus clowns are Leon "Buttons" McBryde and Steve "T. J. Tatters" Smith. I met both of them through my relationship with Mark Anthony. Leon is a very tall man with a heart larger than his body and a love for people rooted in the gospel of Jesus Christ. He is a wonderful example of an Epiphany clown. When Steve Smith was the dean of Ringling Bros. and Barnum & Bailey's Clown College, I said that he was the best performing clown in America. These two men's tremendous energy, love, and respect for their audiences, and creative, exaggerated pictures of human weaknesses made them both Hall of Fame clowns.

In Christian clowning the auguste clown can be the country bumpkin who doesn't quite get the whole picture, much like some of the disciples of Jesus. Peter may be the best example of an Epiphany clown. His weaknesses show the grace of God. He is so certain that he is right on any point, that he boldly speaks up and often puts his foot in his mouth. He is so certain that he is right, he even rebukes Jesus when Jesus talked about his suffering and death:

> Then he began to teach them that the Son of Man must undergo great suffering, and be rejected by the elders, the chief priests, and the scribes, and be killed, and after

28 Dick Hardel, *Welcome to the Sawdust Circle Part II, Learning the Art of Clown Ministry*, p. 45.

three days rise again. He said all this quite openly. And Peter took him aside and began to rebuke him. But turning and looking at his disciples, he rebuked Peter and said, "Get behind me, Satan! For you are setting your mind not on divine things but on human things."
(Mark 8:31-33)

Like an auguste clown, Peter is often puzzled. So he boldly asks Jesus questions in a way that might make him look wise to others. But Jesus' response clearly shows that Peter didn't get it.

Then Peter came and said to him, "Lord, if another member of the church sins against me, how often should I forgive? As many as seven times?" Jesus said to him, "Not seven times, but I tell you, seventy-seven times." *(Matthew 18:21-22)*

Like an auguste clown, when Peter steps out in faith he trips and falls. He must have brought many smiles and laughter to Jesus. Even his best attempts at being faithful need God's help, whether walking on water or professing who Jesus is:

Peter answered him, "Lord, if it is you, command me to come to you on the water." He said, "Come." So Peter got out of the boat, started walking on the water, and came toward Jesus. But when he noticed the strong wind, he became frightened, and beginning to sink, he cried out, "Lord save me!" Jesus immediately reached out his hand and caught him, saying to him, "You of little faith, why did you doubt?" When they got into the boat, the wind ceased. And those in the boat worshiped him, saying, "Truly you are the Son of God."
(Matthew 14:28-33)

He said to them, "But who do you say that I am?" Simon Peter answered, "You are the Messiah, the Son of the living God." And Jesus answered him, "Blessed are you Simon son of Jonah! For flesh and blood has not revealed this to you, but my Father in heaven." *(Matthew 16:15-17)*

When Jesus shares with the disciples how all of them will abandon him when he begins his suffering and journey to the cross, Peter boldly proclaims that the others might desert Jesus, but he will never leave Jesus. How painful that look of Jesus must have been after Peter had denied Jesus in the courtyard where Jesus was brought to the high priest for trial.

Peter said to him, "Though all become deserters because of you, I will never desert you." Jesus said to him, "Truly I tell you, this very night, before the cock crows, you will deny me three times. Peter said to him, "Even though I must die with you, I will not deny you." And so said all the disciples. *(Matthew 26:33-35)*

Then he began to curse, and he swore an oath, "I do not know the man!" At that moment the cock crowed. Then Peter remembered what Jesus had said: "Before the cock crows, you will deny me three times." And he went out and wept bitterly. *(Matthew 26:74-75)*

Like one clown gag after another, Peter with James and John fell asleep, just when Jesus needed them at a most crucial time. The picture of this gospel story is much like a member of the pastor's family snoring loudly while the pastor is preaching.

Then he came to the disciples and found them sleeping; and he said to Peter, "So, could you not stay awake with me one hour? Stay awake and pray that you may not come into the time of trial; the spirit indeed is willing, but the flesh is weak." Again he went away for the second time and prayed, "My Father, if this cannot pass unless I drink it, your will be done." Again he came and found them sleeping, for their eyes were heavy. So leaving them again, he went away and prayed for the third time, saying the same words. Then he came to the disciples and said to them, "Are you still sleeping and taking your rest? See, the hour is at hand and the Son of Man is betrayed into the hands of sinners. *(Matthew 26:40-45)*

Upon hearing the news of the empty tomb from Mary Magdalene, Peter and John had a race to the graveyard. His large clown shoes must have slowed him down as he tripped his way to the empty tomb.

Then Peter and the other disciple set out and went toward the tomb. The two were running together, but the other disciple outran Peter and reached the tomb first. He bent down to look in and saw the linen wrappings lying there, but he did not go in. Then Simon Peter came, following him, and went into the tomb. He saw the linen wrappings lying there, and the cloth that had been on Jesus' head, not lying with the linen wrappings but rolled up in a place by itself. Then the other disciple, who reached the tomb first, also went in, and he saw and believed, for as yet they did not understand the scripture, that he must rise from the dead. Then the disciples returned to their homes. (John 20:3-10)

How painful it must have been for Peter, after the resurrection, to hear Jesus ask him three times, whether Peter loved him (John 21:15-19).

The book of Acts records the difficulty Peter had in understanding that the gospel is to be proclaimed to Gentiles as well as the Jews. God almost had to hit him over the head with a two-by-four before Peter understood that God showed no partiality in his foolish plan of salvation:

Now while Peter was greatly puzzled about what to
make of the vision that he had seen, suddenly the men
sent by Cornelius appeared. *(Acts 10:17)*

Then Peter began to speak to them: "I truly understand
that God shows no partiality, but in every nation anyone
who fears him and does what is right is acceptable to
him. *(Acts 10:34-35)*

Like the Epiphany clown, the auguste, Peter often gets to
"Uh-oh!" in his boldness of acting out faith in Jesus Christ. He
occasionally comes to "Ah," when he beholds the glory of God
in Jesus, but he rarely gets to "A-ha!" His strength of boldness
becomes his greatest weakness. But God's strength and foolish
plan are seen through Peter's weakness.

It is the Spirit of God, the life-giver who gives the auguste
clown the full picture. The Epiphany clown has a strong foundation of faith, but doesn't know many answers. Faith always seeks
understanding so the Epiphany clown searches for meaning—
"What does this mean?" Looking at life through the cross of
Christ the auguste clown in Christian clowning searches for rays
of God's glory. This clown is certain that God's grace will always
bring a surprise, even when he may trip and fall! The whole character of the auguste clown in ministry is totally dependent on the
grace of God.

The auguste clown in ministry sees the world upside-down
and knows that she cannot turn it right-side-up. So she trusts the
grace and power of God manifest in Jesus, the Christ, and creates
word pictures of the glory of God. The surprise of God's grace is
that sometimes the auguste clown gets a glimpse of life right-
side-up, and it looks like the following prayer:

Lord, make us instruments of your peace.
Where there is hatred, let us sow love;
Where there is injury, pardon;
Where there is discord, union;

Where there is doubt, faith;
Where there is despair, hope;
Where there is darkness, light;
Where there is sadness, joy.
Grant that we may not so much seek
To be consoled as to console;
To be understood as to understand;
To be loved as to love.
For it is in giving that we receive;
It is in pardoning that we are pardoned; and
It is in dying that we are born to eternal life.

—Prayer Attributed to St. Francis[29]

Three Clown Types
Together in One Ministry

At this the whole earth exults in boundless joy.[30]

On Pentecost the believers are both gathered and sent. They are
gathered into a holy community in the name of Jesus Christ and
sent out into mission to the world in the name of Jesus Christ.
They were empowered by the outpouring of the Holy Spirit. The
message of the resurrection of Jesus Christ is one that the whole
earth exults in with boundless joy. The themes of the Pentecost
season of the church year are the best way to describe the ministry of Christian clowning. In the name of Jesus Christ all the
clown types are gathered and they are sent out into the world to
use the uniqueness of their character and gifts so that others are
touched by the gospel. Pentecost joins the three clown types into
one ministry.

Pentecost is very much like families, children of all ages,
gathered at a picnic to play the game of salvation tag. God gathers the people and touches each of them with the good news of
salvation in Jesus Christ. Through this good message the Holy

---

29 *Lutheran Book of Worship*, p. 48.

30 From the Preface for the Liturgy of the Festival of Pentecost, *Lutheran Book of
Worship, Minister's Desk Edition* (Minneapolis: Augsburg Publishing House,
1978), p. 215.

Spirit empowers all the people to play salvation tag. Upon hearing the good news, the people are filled with joy. God says, "Go! Proclaim! Make disciples! Baptize! Teach! You're it!" Filled with joy, the people scatter to their homes and neighborhoods to touch others with the good news of salvation so that they can be "It!" They continue to gather regularly to rest and catch their breath, then they go out again to touch others. Through the Spirit, Christ is always present when they gather and when they go. It's a game they play for the rest of their lives.

Herb Brokering has written a wonderful parable about a Pentecost ministry of telling the story. Christ clowns always tell the story.

Once upon a time there were children who wanted to know how God's rules began. They heard true stories of people who had been saved from slavery and oppression, who were guided through a great sea, and saved from death before a mighty army. So great was the story of this salvation that the children memorized it and then taught it to their children. Many generations later the story is still alive, and retold to children's children. It is memorized, whispered around bonfires to families, written in a great book, and preserved in songs. The story is the preamble for all rules. People stand when the big book is opened, where the story of saving them is recorded. They stay standing for the reading of the rules that are written in the same book, just after the saving story. First, they read the good story; then they read the good rules. The good news and the good rules cannot be separated from each other.[31]

Pentecost is a major festival of the Christian church that comes fifty days after Easter. The word *Pentecost* comes from the Greek translation of the Old Testament, called the Septuagint,

31 Herb Brokering, Dick Hardel, and Penne Sewall, *Tag, You're It!* (Minneapolis: Youth & Family Institute of Augsburg College, 1998), p. 221.

meaning "the fiftieth day." The festival was so named because it fell on the fiftieth day after the ceremony of the barley sheaf during the Passover observances. But much like Herb Brokering's parable, the Christian festival has roots in the Jewish tradition. The original day of Pentecost fell on the days of the Jewish festival, the Feast of Weeks. In Exodus 34:22 we learn that the festival is a gathering of the first fruits of the harvest. It was a national thanksgiving to God festival. As it is described in Deuteronomy 16:9-11 we learn that the Jewish families were to

give thanks to God, as God had blessed them and they were to rejoice. So the Jewish festival of Pentecost or Weeks was filled with rejoicing.[32]

The New Testament celebration of Pentecost has its roots in the Jewish themes of thanksgiving and rejoicing. The Holy Spirit empowers the people of God to tell the story of God's foolish plan of salvation. The story of salvation in Jesus Christ is one that calls

32 George A. Buttrick, editor, *The Interpreter's Dictionary of the Bible* (Nashville, Tennessee: Abingdon Press, 1962), Vol. 4, pp.827-828.

for the whole earth to rejoice. The liturgical color for the feast of
Pentecost is red, representing the fiery flames on the heads of
those who received the Holy Spirit as recorded in Acts 2.

> Divided tongues, as of fire, appeared among them, and
> a tongue rested on each of them. All of them were filled
> with the Holy Spirit and began to speak in other lan-
> guages, as the Spirit gave them ability. (Acts 2:3-4)

Pentecost is a time of spiritual renewal through the good
news of Jesus Christ. It is a festival of the church to remind and
empower the people of God to be on fire for the gospel. It is a
gathering to remind believers that they are sent out by God to
rejoice in the Lord, to proclaim the gospel and serve people with
the love of God. By taking a close look at the festival of
Pentecost, Christ clowns can see how the unique gifts of the three
clown types blend into one ministry. It is a ministry that connects
the cross and the sawdust circle.

The various scripture lessons for Pentecost always stress the
empowerment of the Holy Spirit in a believer's life. The two
options for Prayer of the Day as well as the Alleluia Verse, used
between the second lesson and the gospel reading, focus on the
people of God with hearts on fire for the gospel.

Two Options for the Prayer of the Day on Pentecost

*God, the Father of our Lord Jesus Christ, as you sent upon the
disciples the promised gift of the Holy Spirit, look upon your
church and open our hearts to the power of the Spirit. Kindle in
us the fire of your love, and strengthen our lives for service in
your kingdom; through your Son, Jesus Christ our Lord, who
lives and reigns with you in the unity of the Holy Spirit, one
God, now and forever. Amen*

*God our creator, earth has many languages, but your gospel
announces your love to all nations in one heavenly speech.
Make us messengers of the good news, that through the power*

of your Spirit, everyone everywhere may unite in one song of praise; through your Son, Jesus Christ our Lord, who lives and reigns with you in the unity of the Holy Spirit, one God, now and forever. Amen

Alleluia Verse (from Psalm 104:30)

Alleluia. Come, Holy Spirit, fill the hearts of your faithful people, set them on fire with your love. Alleluia.[33]

Clowns in ministry are Pentecost clowns. Renewal in the Holy Spirit is essential for clown ministry. Clowns in ministry must regularly gather with the people of God around Word and sacraments to be renewed and empowered as they are sent out into the world to paint word pictures of the gospel and touch people with the love of God. Full of the life-giving breath of the Holy Spirit, the Pentecost clowns share the joy of salvation and invite others to join them in the foolishness of God as they play, "Tag, You're It!"

Faith is a gift of the Holy Spirit. It is the Holy Spirit who converts people to faith in Jesus Christ. Neither clowns, pastors, teachers, evangelists, nor lay people convert anyone to faith. The Scripture lesson in Acts clearly states the ministry of the Pentecost clowns and the work of the Holy Spirit.

So those who welcomed his message were baptized, and that day about three thousand persons were added. They devoted themselves to the apostles' teaching and fellowship, to the breaking of bread and the prayers. Awe came upon everyone, because many wonders and signs were being done by the apostles. All who believed were together and had all things in common; they would sell their possessions and goods and distribute the proceeds to all, as any had need. Day by day, as they spent much time together in the temple, they broke

---

33 *Lutheran Book of Worship, Minister's Desk Edition* (Minneapolis: Augsburg Publishing House, 1978), p. 158.

bread at home and ate their food with glad and gener-
ous hearts, praising God and having the goodwill of all
the people. And day by day the Lord added to their
number those who were being saved. *(Acts 2:41-47)*

Luther's explanation to the third article of the Apostle's
Creed helps the Pentecost clowns to understand the empowerment of the Holy Spirit:

I believe in the Holy Spirit, the holy catholic [Christian,
universal] church, the communion of saints, the forgiveness of sins, the resurrection of the body, and the life
everlasting. Amen

WHAT DOES THIS MEAN?
ANSWER: I believe that by my own reason or strength I
cannot believe in Jesus Christ, my Lord, or come to him.
But the Holy Spirit has called me through the Gospel,
enlightened me with his gifts, and sanctified and preserved me in true faith, just as he calls, gathers, enlightens, and sanctifies the whole Christian church on earth
and preserves it in union with Jesus Christ in the one
true faith. In this Christian church he daily and abundantly forgives all my sins, and the sins of all believers,
and on the last day he will raise me and all the dead
and will grant eternal life to me and to all who believe
in Christ. This is most certainly true.[34]

Tramp clowns, whiteface clowns, and auguste clowns have
different characteristics and gifts, but they use their different gifts
in one ministry of the gospel. They understand that the cross in
the sawdust circle is not ministry apart from the church, but
rather a ministry of the church. Pentecost clowns know that their
ministry of the gospel is a very important ministry of the church.

34 Theodore G. Tappert, editor, The Book of Concord, (St. Louis, Mo.: Concordia
   Publishing House, 1959), p.345. Again, Luther wrote the Small Catechism in
   1529 and it was included in the Book of Concord of 1580.

But clown ministry is no more important than other tools of proclaiming the gospel. The Holy Spirit first calls us into a community of believers through Jesus Christ. The different gifts and different assignments of ministry work within the community of faith. So pastor, teacher, clown, evangelist, early childhood specialist, youth worker, professional or lay volunteer all use their different gifts in one ministry of the gospel.

> I therefore, the prisoner in the Lord, beg you to lead a life worthy of the calling to which you have been called, with all humility and gentleness, with patience, bearing with one another in love, making every effort to maintain the unity of the Spirit in the bond of peace. There is one body and one Spirit, just as you were called to the one hope of your calling, one Lord, one faith, one baptism, one God and Father of all, who is above all and through all and in all. *(Ephesians 4:1-6)*

This is such an important concept of the church. All the different styles of ministry in the Christian church work for and with one another. Through Christ we are all called into the fellowship of a messianic community. I have seen clowns in ministry who proclaim Jesus but do not gather regularly in the circle of the fellowship of believers. That type ministry easily becomes self-centered and an end unto itself. I have seen the various types of clowns arguing with one another, just like the disciples, about who is the greatest when it comes to costume, makeup, character, and routines. As Jesus said to his disciples, whoever wants to be great in the kingdom of God must become the slave of all, so Pentecost clowns live out the fire of the Holy Spirit by simply serving others in love. The following hymn describes the one ministry of the three clown types so well:

> Jesu, Jesu, fill us with your love,
> show us how to serve
> the neighbors we have from you.

Loving puts us on our knees,
serving as though we are slaves,
this is the way we should live with you.

Kneel at the feet of our friends,
silently washing their feet,
this is the way we should live with you.[35]

Pentecost clowns understand that they are called into the sawdust circle by Christ. The cross stands firmly in the center of the sawdust circle. The essentials for the sawdust circle are proclamation of the gospel, fellowship, and servanthood. As Pentecost clowns focus on those three essentials, they grow in faith and day by day God adds to the number of members of the body of Christ.

---

35 Refrain and verses 4 & 5 from the hymn "Jesu, Jesu, Fill Us with Your Love," written by Tom Colvin in 1963. In *Renew! Songs & Hymns for Blended Worship* (Carol Stream, Ill.: Hope Publishing Co., 1995), #289.

clown ministry in Conclusion

Moving into the 21st century brings new challenges to the church and to the circus. Both have survived such cultural shifts in the past. But never has the challenge been more to reach the audience of the new generations. Because of the emphasis on health and exercise in this new century, and because of greater medical knowledge and practice, people are living longer. Both the church and the circus must reach out and communicate to all the generations, "children of all ages."

I know that the church will not die in the 21st century because Jesus is Lord of the church. It may take some very different forms and direction, but it will not die. There may be many smaller congregations that close their doors because people have moved out of that community, but Jesus will never close his arms. The ministry of the Christian church is to invite people into the arms of Jesus. The church must use every gift of the Holy Spirit to extend the invitation.

Throughout this book I have suggested that the church can learn much from the circus. I believe clowns are a symbol of invitation that the church can use in this new century.

Almost every culture has had some form of clown entertainment. Perhaps human beings have an innate need to laugh at themselves and at others. Good clowns play with the tensions and conflicts that are part of human interaction. This provides a healthy, enlightening, and entertaining experience....

However, good professional clowns are highly disciplined artists who spend a lifetime at their craft, and to this craft they add their intuitive or learned insights about human nature.[1]

It has often been written that the circus clown is dying out with the traditions of the past. The circus is making many changes and it may be a very foolish assumption to think that the traditional circus will die. But the need for the clown and the role of the clown will be with humankind through all the centuries. The clown is the Renaissance Man. It may be that there is more room in the church for clowns than in the new circuses. As Kenneth Feld closed Clown College for the circus, the church might open its Christ Clown College. I can see it now:

Join the Ecclesiastical Extravaganza

Concordia Christ Clown College, the
Christian Clown Connection
of the 21st Century

Join Jocular Jocose Jokers In A Jovial Jaunt Of Jubilant Jesting On Justification Spotlighting Sidesplitting Shenanigans And Spontaneous Skylarking In The Simply Silliness And Senselessness Of The Plan of Salvation

And the Foolishness of God,
The Lord of Laughter!

The cross in the sawdust circle provides many new angles of insight to the love of God that has always been open and offered free of charge. "Foolish!" you may say. But in the midst of peo-

1 Mark Stolzenberg, *Clown for Circus & Stage* (New York: Sterling Publishing Co., 1982), p. 151.

ple who shout, "Stupid! Foolish! Impossible! Ridiculous!" the clown takes the risk of faith and lives life inside-out, thus exposing the heart of the gospel to people. Through Christ the people of God are filled with "ooh"s and "aah"s and "ha! ha! ha!"s. From the cross in the sawdust circle the clown can see signs of promise even in the tears of life. The clown leads Christ's parade of "already but not yet," of "once you were but now you are," of law and gospel, of sin and grace, from darkness into light, from death to resurrection! The clown, balanced with one foot in faith and the other in fantasy, walks among the people and teaches them to play "Tag, You're It!" with the gospel. The clown does not stick around for applause or thanks. Love and laughter are given away by the clown with each word picture she creates, whether or not people say thank you.

What does an author say at the close of a book? What does a clown say at the end of a show? In my research I found this wonderful quote of the closing dialog between French clowns Emile Recordier (1890–1946) and Alphonse Boullicot (1887–1957) that answers the questions so well:

"What do you say to the public at the end of the show?"

"What do you say to the public, my dear Mimile? You say goodbye of course!"

"WRONG Boullicot! You never say goodbye to the public, you say: Here's to the next time!"[2]

The recessional parade leaves the hippodrome and goes into the world of the 21st century to present the foolishness of God in Christ, *The Greatest Show On Earth*! Can you hear the kazoos and the singing?

We are marching in the light of God,
We are marching in the light of God,

2 Howard Loxton, *The Golden Age of the Circus* (New York: Smithmark Publishers, 1997), p. 111.

We are marching in the light of God,
We are marching in the light of God,
We are marching, we are marching—ooh, ooh—we are
marching in the light of God.
We are marching, we are marching—ooh, ooh—we are
marching in the light of God.[3]

May All Your Days Be Circus Days
For Life In Christ Is A Circus!

---

3 Zulu traditional song from South Africa, *With One Voice* (Minneapolis: Augsburg
   Fortress, 1995), #650.

Appendix: Clown Ministry in Worship

I am including here an example of how this theology of clown ministry is visualized in a worship service. The worship service that follows was written by Heather "Sparkplug" Hultgren and myself for a Sunday worship service at Mt. Carmel Retreat Center. The clowns and I were asked to lead a family camp weekend on the healing power of laughter and play. Heather is the boss clown of the Eagan, Minnesota, Unit of the Life In Christ Circus.

I do not like to do an entire clown worship service unless all the members of the audience or congregation are clowns. Rather, I suggest that it is more effective to use the regular liturgy of the people and do some divine interruptions. These are *interruptions*, not *disruptions*. Disruptions force people to worship in a form that is not theirs and it may make them very uncomfortable and, perhaps, angry. Interruptions value the liturgy or form of worship that is common with the members of a specific congregation, but call for a *time out* to take a second look at what was just done. Divine interruptions should create a picture of what is valued and stated in a specific section of the liturgy. Divine interruptions are excellent tools for teaching the liturgy or the meaning of a text of scripture.

The key to exciting worship is to build on the theme of the scripture texts for a specific Sunday or other holy day. It is best to use two to four clowns to help plan a worship service. One of the people should know the theology and the liturgical practice of the people who will be attending the worship service. The planners must know the scripture texts well, the traditions of the Christian church well, and the audience well. Clowns, circus people, and Christian leaders should know that worship should be intergenerational—it should affirm "children of all ages."

The setting for this worship service was a large chapel at a camp or retreat center. This chapel could hold about 300 people. All the furniture was easily movable. We set up the chancel and the nave exactly as it was normally set for a Sunday worship service. Although the chapel had its own sound system, we still used our sound system to play the background music to the clown routines.

The lessons for the 12th Sunday after Pentecost were taken from the Revised Common Lectionary, Series C. The liturgical color for this Sunday was green. It is a season of growth through the outpouring of the Holy Spirit. The theme for the worship service came from the lessons. Jesus is the mediator of a new covenant. Through Jesus, one sees a clearer picture of God and of the laws for God's people. The theme for this worship service is the ministry of Jesus on the Sabbath. According to the old covenant, the people of God were commanded to observe the sabbath day and to keep it holy. In Deuteronomy 5:12-16 we are shown that the key understanding is not to simply remember and observe a specific day, but to remember who God is in our lives. This means to set aside time from our busy schedules to rest in the presence of our God. But just like the Pharisees at the time of Jesus, we can easily focus on keeping the letter of the law and miss the meaning. It is possible for a person to attend a worship service of a congregation, only to say she or he attended, and yet fail to rest in the presence of God. To help visualize this point we cut about ten feet of white butcher paper and glued on large blue letters spelling "SABBATH." Next we cut out clown footprints and glued them on to give the look that the sign had been trampled upon. We also painted tire tracks over the sign. The sign was placed on the floor in front of the altar before the service, and all the clown routines for this service were done on the sign. We even had a baptism in the second worship service, and we moved the baptismal font on top of the sign so that even the baptism was done on the Sabbath. The sign was carried out by the clowns during the recessional and placed on the floor connecting the nave and the narthex so that as people left worship, they all journeyed home on the Sabbath.

You will see in the printed order of service (beginning on page 190 of this book) that we highlighted the major point of each scripture lesson in boldface. Following the reading of each scripture lesson the clowns created a picture of the main point. At the end of the clown routine the clowns stood in a frozen position until the lector read the section in boldface again. There are many more things the worship planning team may choose to do in the worship service.

The following are explanations of the various parts of the worship service. I share these as examples. The printed order of service begins on page 190.

Pre-Service Music

One could use traditional circus music or traditional church music. I like using both to connect the cross and the sawdust circle. The music should help people focus on what is to come and the meaning of the theme for the day.

Worship Warm-Up

Help people learn the melodies for new songs. We prepared a kit for each person. The worship kit was a brown paper lunch bag containing a kazoo, a roll of streamer confetti, the worship folder or bulletin, and one of four types of whistle (slide whistle, train whistle, whirly whistle, or gym whistle). During worship warm-up we practiced singing some of the songs to be used during worship. We also told the people when we would use the kazoos, the whistles, and confetti. We taught the people how to use a kazoo. We even practiced using harmony with the kazoos.

Invocation

We call upon the name of our Triune God and we state that we believe in the foolishness of God's plan of salvation. That is the very reason why we gathered together—to worship and thank God, to be strengthened and renewed in faith, and to go out in the name of our God and practice our faith.

Confession/Absolution

After the pastor announces the good news of forgiveness, the people and the pastor are seated. The following divine interruption creates a picture of what the pastor and people had just done. The purpose of the divine interruption is to highlight the action of the liturgy, which too often has become so familiar that the people do not even remember the importance of the act.

A clown (could be any of the three types; perhaps a tramp clown might be best) enters the chancels, stands in front of the altar facing the people. The clown makes the sign of the cross just as the pastor had done, looks at people and with a very puzzled look scratches his head and shrugs his shoulders as if to ask, "What does that mean?" Suddenly the clown gets an idea, and with delight lets the people in on it. The clown waves to a group of about eight to ten other clowns to come forward from the back of the nave. As soon as the lead clown waves the other clowns forward, the sound person begins a CD recording of ragtime music. Each of the other clowns have a broom, dust mop, a feather duster, or a cleaning cloth. As they come forward they dust off the sin from the people and sweep it toward the lead clown standing in the chancel. The lead clown then takes a dustpan and holds it high in the air for all the people to see. The huge ball of collected sin is brushed together and onto the dustpan. The lead clown shows the people the boundaries of the large ball of sin. Now the lead clown tries to find a hiding place for the dust ball of sin. Each time the lead clown tries to hide the ball the other clowns stomp their feet and wave their arms to express "No!" The lead clown may try to hide the dust ball of sin in some of the plants in the chancel, or in the baptismal font, or in the pastor's vestments, or under the fair linen on the altar. Perplexed as to where to hide the dust ball of sin, the lead clown discovers a cross (which was positioned earlier by or behind the altar), picks up the cross, and pours all the gathered sin into the cross so that it totally disappears into the cross. The lead clown puts down the dustpan and holds the cross high so that all the people can see. The lead clown makes the sign of the cross using his hand just as the pastor had done, looks at the people, and smiles. It is an "A-ha!"

Psalmody

It is very good for people of God to read the psalms. But people should also mediate upon them. In worship some people chant the psalms. They often use the key verse of the psalmody to be the antiphon. The antiphon may be repeated several times during the psalm. It is important for the people of God to *do* the psalms as well as listen to or read them. So I suggest that with certain psalms specific actions be given to the people and be used as the antiphon. Psalm 103:1-8 is used for the psalmody for the 12th Sunday after Pentecost. It describes who God is. Divide the people who have come to worship into four parts. The person reading the psalm will read only two verses and then say, "The Lord is...." The first group will immediately stand up, lift hands high and out, then bring their hands to their hearts and say together, "Merciful." Then they will sit down.

Immediately the second group will stand and, making a gesture with their hands going from their hearts to an outreach or giving position, they say, "Gracious." Then they sit down.

Immediately the third group stands and, moving their arms like a runner in very slow motion and speaking in slow motion, say, "S-l-o-w t-o a-n-g-e-r." Then they sit down.

Immediately the fourth group stands, picks up the pace by jumping up and down and saying quickly, "And abounding in steadfast love!" Then they sit down.

This style uses an active learning process and it is a fun way of doing the psalm. This picture of who God is will be remembered by all the people.

Faithful Family Song

Since this was a worship service designed for Sunday worship following a Christian family weekend, Heather and I wrote new words to the verses of the hymn "Earth and All Stars!"[1]

Old Testament Lesson: Isaiah 58:9-14

The point of this clown routine is that we should not trample on the Sabbath day by pursuing our own interests. Remember that the large "SABBATH" sign is on the floor. All the clown routines are done on this sign. One of the clowns runs to the other side of the stage or chancel over the "SABBATH" sign without ever seeing it. She is carrying another sign. She holds it up to reveal: CLOWN SALE! Then she loudly calls a group of about seven other clowns over. "Clown sale! Clown sale! Everything a clown needs." The remaining seven clowns also run across the chancel, over the "SABBATH" sign, to the clown sale. They continue to talk about all the wonderful things they wish to purchase. Two tramp clowns enter last, look at all the other clowns at the clown sale, then look down at the "SABBATH" sign, and pick up the "SABBATH" sign so that all the people in worship can see the tire marks and the footprints. When the sign is raised, the other clowns at the sale stop talking and look at the sign. The two tramp clowns say, "Oh! Oh!" All the clowns stay in a frozen position until the lector reads the boldface section of the scripture passage. Then the tramp clowns place the "SABBATH" sign back on the floor of the chancel and the clowns exit.

1 "Earth and All Stars," Text: Herbert E. Brokering, b. 1926. Tune: David N. Johnson, b. 1922. From *Lutheran Book of Worship* (Minneapolis: Augsburg Publishing House, 1978), #558.

Epistle Lesson: Hebrews 12:18-29

The book of Hebrews uses some difficult language for people who are not familiar with the imagery of the Old Testament stories. The point in this text is that through Jesus Christ we move into a new covenant. Christ is the mediator of the new covenant. We no longer have to fear God. Jesus turns the world upside-down.

Enter a clown who is the Christ figure for this routine. He stands on the "SABBATH" sign, stretches out his arms and hangs his head downward as the crucified Jesus hanging on the cross. He is wearing a kingly crown. An auguste clown enters and looks at the Christ figure but sees the resurrected Christ as well as the crucified Christ. The auguste clown sees a different picture of Christ, runs to the corner of the chancel, picks up two huge white gloves (like Mickey Mouse gloves), and puts one glove on each hand at the end of the "cross." The auguste clown smiles and exits. The Christ figure clown, with arms still extended, motions with gloved hands for two clowns to enter from opposite sides of the cross. Each of these two clowns carries a sign. One sign says "LAW"; the other, "GOSPEL." The two clowns walk to the extended arms of the Christ figure, the cross, and stop. They are facing the people. The Christ figure clown motions with the white gloves that they are to move in closer. The clowns move in closer and stand right next to each other, and the arms of the cross wrap around them and move them to hug each other. They hug and smile at the people. The arms of the cross open again and they walk off together, both smiling and showing the signs connected. The Christ figure clown remains standing in the cross position, but now smiles and raises the arms toward heaven, while the lector reads the section of Hebrews in boldface. Repeat, using other clowns with different signs reading: Fear/Love; Light/Darkness; Sin/Grace; and Death/Resurrection.

Gospel Lesson: Luke 13:10-17

The point of this gospel reading is that Jesus is more important than the letter of the law. The Pharisees keep the letter of the law, but miss the point. Jesus heals on the Sabbath. Again this activity takes place on the "SABBATH" sign. The same clown that played the Christ figure in the epistle lesson comes out and sits on a chair positioned on the sign. Behind the Christ figure clown is a large sign that says "CURRATOR" (meaning one who cures or heals). Two auguste clowns read the sign and understand that Jesus cures, so they quickly bring a couple of rubber chickens and rubber pigs to be cured for the picnic meal. Jesus smiles at them but waves them off. Another female clown enters from the opposite side of the chancel. She can barely walk. She uses a cane and is bent over. The Christ figure clown stands up, walks over to her, looks at her with compassion, and touches her back. Immediately the female clown stands up straight, lifts her hands up in praise, and loudly sings, "Rise! Shine! And give God the glory, glory! Rise! Shine! And give God the glory, glory!"

Enter two whiteface clowns, who, like the Pharisees, do everything by the letter of the law. They stand at opposite sides of the Christ figure clown and each points a finger at Jesus in an accusing way. They begin to shake their fingers at Jesus to indicate that he has done something terribly wrong. The Christ figure clown shrugs his shoulders and with a puzzled look indicates, "Now what's wrong?" The whiteface clowns point to the "SABBATH" sign and indicate that Jesus should not be curing people on the Sabbath. It is wrong! The Christ figure clown points to the female clown who has been cured. Immediately she breaks out into another chorus, "Rise! Shine! And give God the glory, glory! Rise! Shine! And give God the glory, glory!" The two whiteface clowns turn away, cover their ears, and walk away. The Christ figure clown and the clown who has been healed remain in the chancel before the altar, facing the people. They freeze with a smile on their faces while the lector reads the part of the lesson in boldface. At the end of the reading the two exit, walking arm in arm.

Gospel Song

Again, I wrote new words to the old hymn tune, "I Know That My Redeemer Lives!"[2] The words connect the foolishness of God's plan of salvation with the Easter message in August. Kazoos are used for the second verse. After singing the third verse, the worship leader counts with the people, "One, Two, Three," then they all shout, "Alleluia!" and throw the streamers of confetti.

Offering (divine interruption)

After the ushers have received the offering and the pastor has presented the gifts before the altar, a clown walks up the aisle of the nave from the back toward the altar. The clown is carrying a wash tub (large enough to stand in). The clown walks up to the altar carrying the tub, looks at the gifts in the offering plate and then sadly looks at the people. The clown shows the people that tub is empty. Next the clown places the tub on the "SABBATH" sign before the altar. The clown begins to look for some dollars to give or something significant to give as an offering, but has nothing to offer. The clown thinks and thinks and looks and looks only to discover that the clown has nothing. Suddenly, the clown gets the idea and expresses to the people an "A-ha!" The clown turns around facing the altar and steps into the tub with both feet. The clown raises her arms up toward the heavens. Then the clown waves at two other clowns, inviting them to join her and step into the tub, offering themselves to God also. After the third clown steps into the tub, the other two join hands on each side of the third clown and freeze in that position until the pastor completes the offertory prayer. After the prayer the clowns exit, taking the wash tub with them.

> Gracious God, with joy we offer ourselves to the ministry of your kingdom. We rededicate our lives to serving

2 "I Know That My Redeemer Lives!" Text by Samuel Medley, 1738–99. Tune by John Hatton, died 1793. From *Lutheran Book of Worship* (Minneapolis: Augsburg Publishing House, 1978), #352.

you. Consecrate our lives so that we may proclaim your love in everything we do during this coming week. Pour out your Holy Spirit upon us and empower us to live fully dedicated to you. We offer our bodies, souls, spirits, and all our possessions for the sake of Jesus Christ who died for us all. Amen

Response of Praise and Thanksgiving (from Psalm 150)

The key phrase of this psalm is "let everything that has breath, praise the Lord. The psalmist suggests different instruments for the people of God to use. We use the different type of whistles because they all take breath. It is important to remind the people, especially the children, that they are only to blow the whistle when the pastor or worship leader calls for their whistle as written in the worship folder.

Alleluia Balloons

This is doing the parable of Herb Brokering printed on page 1 this book. Depending of the number of people in the worship service, the clowns will bring twenty to thirty balloons into the nave and stand among the people. The pastor or a worship leader reads the parable. Then the leader instructs the people to keep all the balloons floating in the air. They should not talk during this time, except for when they hit a balloon, at which point they should they say, "Alleluia!" This creates a picture of the color of praise to God. The worship leaders should instruct the people to hit the balloons and fill the air with "Alleluia!"'s until they hear the train whistle. When the leader blows the train whistle, whoever is close to a balloon should grab the balloon and break it by sitting on it. It is worship with a bang! (And the balloons are broken to keep the people from continuously playing with them.)

Clown Benediction

The props needed for this blessing routine are five large grocery bags or shopping bags with handles, each containing a very large heart cut out of red paper or cloth and about 75 heart stickers with the words "God loves you!" or "Jesus loves you!" (enough stickers for each worshipper to receive one, divided among the five bags). The bags are closed and stacked, lying flat upon each other on a chair.

Soft, gentle, background music begins. The first clown enters, looks at the bags, then looks with wonder at the people. The clown shrugs the shoulders and walks to one side of the chancel area.

Then a second clown enters, looks at the bags, picks up a bag, but never opens it. The second clown goes to the opposite end of the chancel from the first clown.

A third clown enters, looks at bags, picks one up, opens it, and discovers that there is a large heart. That clown shows it to the people but begins to hoard the heart. The clown continues to hoard the heart and walks near the first clown and remains standing there.

Enter the fourth clown. This clown looks at the bags, picks one up, opens it, discovers the heart, shows it to the people, but begins to flaunt it. None of the first four clowns know what to do with the heart.

Enter the fifth clown, possibly a tramp clown, the least likely to bear good news. The tramp clown looks at the bag, picks it up, opens it, and pulls out the large heart. The tramp clown looks at the people, then the heart, and back at the people and knows exactly what to do with the heart—give it away. The tramp clown walks down the center aisle to the middle and begins to give the heart stickers to the people. As soon as the other clowns see what the tramp clown has done, they, too, join in giving the love away. The second clown opens her bag and discovers her heart and gives the heart stickers to others. The first clown walks over to the chair and picks up her bag, opens it, and upon discovering the heart, also begins to give her heart stickers away. For a very large gathering of people, other clowns who were not in the routine may join in the handing out of the hearts of blessing until everyone has a heart.

Closing Song

Again, Heather and I wrote new words to an old hymn tune, this time "Beautiful Savior."[3] As the people sing this closing verse, one clown holds up the cross used for the divine interruption of confession and absolution and walks down the center aisle of the nave from the altar to the narthex. The other clowns follow, carrying the "SABBATH" sign. They lay the sign down on the floor for people to walk on as they leave. Everyone walks on the Sabbath as they journey home. Lively music should be played as the people leave worship.

3 "Beautiful Savior," Text: Gesangbuch, Muenster, 1677; translated by Joseph a Seiss, 1823–1904. Tune: Silesian folk tune, 1842. From *Lutheran Book of Worship* (Minneapolis: Augsburg Publishing House, 1978), #518.

Twelfth Sunday after Pentecost

Note to worshippers: The word liturgy *means "work of the people." This worship service is designed for the people of the congregation to be very active. It is visual as well as audible. Each worshipper has been given a worship kit that contains items used in the liturgy. L = Leaders; P = People.*

Pre-Service Music

Worship Warm Up

Invocation

L: Ladies and Gentlemen, Children of All Ages! We begin this worship service on the Sabbath day in the name of our God: Father, + Son, and Holy Spirit—the great Three in One! Throughout the world Christian people remember the Sabbath day and keep it holy.

P: *Yeah, but most people would say, "How foolish!"*

L: Foolish?

P: *Yes, foolish to believe in a God who created the universe when the wisdom of our scientific research seems to tell us of another theory.*

L: Foolish?

P: *Yes, foolish to believe in a God who would rescue and forgive people who continue to trip, fall, and sin in their relationships.*

L: Foolish?

P: *Yes, foolish to believe in a God who continues to gather people into a ho-ho-holy community.*

L: What is foolish about that?

P: *Few believe it because it doesn't make sense to love like God loves!*

L: Well, you are right. This God does not make sense! The cross does not make sense. Grace does not make sense and yet it is the key to our gathering this morning. We believe in the foolishness of God!

Confession/Absolution

L: Because we believe we count on the forgiveness of this gracious God. Let us confess our sins to God:

P: *Most Merciful God, we confess that we are locked up in our sins. We cannot free ourselves. We have sinned against you and against one another. Sometimes we failed to act out of love and faith. We too often have done nothing to help others and witness to your grace. Other times our actions have been selfish. We put ourselves first and you last in our daily living. Forgive us, gracious God. Jesus is the key to unlock us from our sin and set us free. Renew us and lead us to live our lives to your glory. Amen*

L: Christ is the key to open our lives that are locked in sin. Because of Jesus' death and resurrection God forgives all our sins. As a called and ordained minister of the church of Christ and by his authority, I declare to you that we are forgiven in the name of the Father, and of the + Son, and of the Holy Spirit. Amen!

Divine Interruption

Psalmody
Psalm 103:1-8

L: The Lord is...

(Refrain by people)

> *Merciful*
> *Gracious*
> *Slow to anger*
> *And abounding in steadfast love*

Faithful Family Song
(to the tune of "Earth and All Stars")

Refrain: God has done ma-a-a-arv-e-lous things.
         Families shall praise him with their whole hearts!

1. Praise to the Lord!
   People together!
   Sing to the Lord a new song!
   Stand hand in hand.
   Christ's love unites us!
   Sing to the Lord a new song!

2. Children and friends,
   Sounds of the babies,
   Sing to the Lord a new song!
   Run, skip, and play,
   Energy boundless!
   Sing to the Lord a new song!

3. Parents and kids,
   Aunts, uncles, cousins.
   Sing to the Lord a new song!
   Grandparents too!
   With years of wisdom,
   Sing to the Lord a new song!

4. Laughter and play—
   A healthy family.
   Sing to the Lord a new song!
   And when we fall,
   Jesus forgives us!
   Sing to the Lord a new song!

Old Testament Lesson
Isaiah 58: 9-14

Then you shall call, and the Lord will answer; you shall cry for help, and he will say, Here I am. If you remove the yoke from among you, the pointing of the finger, the speaking of evil, if you offer your food to the hungry and satisfy the needs of the afflicted, then your light shall rise in the darkness and your gloom be like the noonday. The Lord will guide you continually, and satisfy your needs in parched places, and make your bones strong; and you shall be like a watered garden, like a spring of water, whose waters never fail. Your ancient ruins shall be rebuild; you shall raise up the foundations of many genera-tions; you shall be called the repairer of the breach, the restor-er of the streets to live in. If you refrain from trampling the sabbath, from pursuing your own interests on my holy day; if you call the sabbath a delight and the holy day of the Lord honorable; if you honor, not going your own ways, serving your own interests, or pursuing your own affairs; then you shall take delight in the Lord, and I will make you ride upon the heights of the earth; I will feed you with the heritage of your ancestor Jacob, for the mouth of the Lord has spoken.

Epistle Lesson
Hebrews 12:18-29

*You have not come to something that can be touched, a blazing fire, and darkness, and gloom, and a tempest, and the sound of a trumpet, and a voice whose words made the hearers beg that not another word be spoken to them. (For they could not endure the order that was given, "If even an animal touches the mountain, it shall be stoned to death." Indeed, so terrifying was the sight that Moses said, "I tremble with fear.") But you have come to Mount Zion and to the city of the living God, the heavenly Jerusalem, and to innumerable angels in festal gathering, and to the assembly of the firstborn who are enrolled in heaven, and to God the judge of all, and to the spirits of the righteous made perfect, **and to Jesus, the mediator of a new covenant, and to the sprinkled blood that speaks a better word than the blood of Abel.***

See that you do not refuse the one who is speaking; for if they did not escape when they refused the one who warned them on earth, how much less will we escape if we reject the one who warns from heaven! At that time his voice shook the earth; but now he has promised, "Yet once more I will shake not only the earth, but also the heaven." This phrase, "Yet once more," indicates the removal of what is shaken—that is, created things—so that what cannot be shaken may remain. Therefore, since we are receiving a kingdom that cannot be shaken, let us give thanks, by which we offer to God an acceptable worship with reverence and awe; for indeed our God is a consuming fire.

Worship service written by Heather Hultgren and Dr. Dick Hardel.

Gospel Lesson
Luke 13:10-17

Now he was teaching in one of the synagogues on the sabbath. And just then there appeared a woman with a spirit that had crippled her for eighteen years. She was bent over and was quite unable to stand up straight. When Jesus saw her, he called her over and said, "Woman, you are set free from your ailment." When he laid his hands on her, immediately she stood up straight and began praising God. But the leader of the synagogue, indignant because Jesus had cured on the sabbath, kept saying to the crowd, "There are six days on which work ought to be done; come on those days and be cured, and not on the sabbath day." But the Lord answered him and said, "You hypocrites! Does not each of you on the sabbath untie his ox or his donkey from the manger, and lead it away to give it water? And ought not this woman, a daughter of Abraham whom Satan bound for eighteen long years, be set free from this bondage on the sabbath day?" When he said this, all his opponents were put to shame; and the entire crowd was rejoicing at all the wonderful things that he was doing.

Gospel Song
(to the tune of "I Know That My Redeemer Lives")

1. Laugh, praise, rejoice so the Scriptures say.
   Jesus has cured on the Sabbath day.
   God has re-de-e-emed us fr-o-om the tomb.
   And set us free from all our gloom!

2. Kazoos

3. Some say we're foolish as we celebrate,
   Easter in August seems so late.
   Picture an A-A-Al-le-lu-u-ia on high
   And throw confetti to the sky!
   (People shout, "Alleluia!" and throw the confetti streamers)

Offering

Divine Interruption

Prayers and Lord's Prayer

Response of Praise (from Psalm 150)

L: Praise the Lord! Praise God in his sanctuary! Praise God with the slide whistles!

P: *(Those with slide whistles blow them then stop.)*

L: Praise him in his mighty firmament! Praise the Lord with the gym whistles!

P: *(Those with gym whistles blow them then stop.)*

L: Praise God for his mighty deeds! Praise the Lord with the whirly whistles!

P: *(Those with whirly whistles blow them then stop.)*

L: Praise God according to his surpassing greatness! Praise the Lord with the train whistles!

P: *(Those with train whistles blow them then stop.)*

L: Praise the Lord with the whirly whistle! *(Blow and stop.)*
Praise the Lord with the slide whistle! *(Blow and stop.)*
Praise the Lord with the train whistle! *(Blow and stop.)*
Praise the Lord with the gym whistle! *(Blow and stop.)*
Let everything that has breath praise the Lord! *(All blow their whistles then stop.)*

Sharing the Peace

Alleluia Balloons

Clown Benediction

Closing Song (to the tune of "Beautiful Savior")

Families to-ge-e-ther, in love for-e-e-ver
Laughter and play on this Sabbath Day!
Jesus is wi-i-th us!
Share love, a family must!
As we go home in joy and hope!

Recessional

L: *Journey home with joy on the Sabbath Day!*

P: *Thanks be to God!*

Glossary: Church & Circus Lingo & Jargon

Ablution: Rinsing the chalice with water after the Communion.

Acolyte: From the Greek "one who follows." Person who lights the candles and carries a torch or candle in a liturgical procession.

Advent: Season that begins the church year, four weeks before Christmas. The liturgical color is blue.

Agnus Dei: From the Latin "Lamb of God." Canticle sung at the distribution of Holy Communion.

After Show: Any show coming after the main performance.

Alb: A white or off-white full-length vestment with sleeves worn in worship by all ranks of ministers, ordained or unordained.

All Out and Over: Entire performance is concluded.

Alleuia: Greek form of the Hebrew hallelujah meaning "Praise the Lord!"

Alms Basin: Large plate on which the offering plates are received from ushers.

Altar: Table on which the Lord's Supper is celebrated. Marking the place of meeting of God and people.

Annie Oakley: Free pass or complimentary ticket.

Anthem: A quasi-liturgical choral composition usually based on Scripture.

Antiphon: A verse from a psalm or other source sung before and after the psalms or canticles for the day.

Antiphonal: A manner of singing alternately by two parts, usually choir and congregation.

Auguste: A type of circus clown apparently introduced by Tom Belling in Berlin in 1869. Wears less makeup than other clown types, has features that are more exaggerated, with white around the eyes. Often the butt end of the jokes and pranks of the whiteface clown. The word *auguste* comes from the Berlin dialect of German meaning "silly" or "stupid."

Back Lot: Area at the rear entrance of the main circus tent, where the animals and trailers are kept.

Badin: A clown figure, often a servant, in medieval French Sotties. Wore white makeup. Was more of a theatrical character and had the gift of banter.

Baggage Stock: Heavy draft or work horses.

Ballyhoo: To attract attention.

Baptistry: Building or area of a building that surrounds the baptismal font. Also a large, pool-sized font for baptisms by immersion.

Banner Line: Canvas paintings in front of the side show.

Benediction: Blessing given at the close of a worship service.

Big Bertha or The Big One: Ringling Bros. and Barnum & Bailey Circus®.

Big Top: The main tent used for the big performance.

Boss Hostler: One in charge of all horses in the show.

Bladder: An animal bladder, usually inflated like a balloon, that is tied to the end of a stick and used as a comic weapon.

Blues: The general admission seats.

Boss Elephant Man: Person in charge of all the elephants.

Boss of Ring Stock: One in charge of performing horses, ponies, etc.

Bulls: Elephants (whether male or female).

Burse: A flat stiff envelope covered with fabric in the color of the season Of the church year in which the corporal and purificators are carried.

Buster: A bad fall. Named after Joseph "Buster" Keaton.

Butcher: Leather-lunged merchant of refreshments.

Canticle: A song, other than a psalm, usually taken from the Bible.

Cantor: A leader of singing.

Carpet Clown: Generally used today to mean a fill-in clown. Historically, a clown who performed on the circus carpet between acts, often getting in the way of ring hands.

Cascadeur: An acrobatic clown who specializes in falls and knockabout comedy.

Cassock: An ankle-length black undergarment with full skirt and long sleeves worn by clergy, choir, musicians, acolytes.

Catholic: Whole, a church that receives the Christian faith intact without alteration or selection of matters of the faith.

Cats: Lions, tigers, leopards, and panthers.

Censer: A closed container in which incense is burned.

Cere Cloth: A cloth the exact size of the top of the altar, treated with wax to resist moisture.

Chalice: A cup used in Holy Communion to contain the wine or grape juice.

Chancel: Space at the liturgically east end of the nave, the altar space.

Chant: From the Latin "to sing." A liturgical song usually sung in unison and unaccompanied, designed to be the bearer of the text.

Chasuble: Poncho-like vestment in the color of the season worn by the presiding minister at Holy Communion.

Cherry Pie: Extra work done by circus employees for extra pay.

Chrism: Mixture of olive oil and a fragrance of balsam used in anointings.

Chrisom: Robe put on one who has been baptized.

Christmas: The Festival of the Holy Nativity, commemorating Christ's birth.

Ciborium: A chalice-shaped vessel with a lid used to hold the bread for Holy Communion.

Cincture: A rope or belt worn around the waist of a cassock or alb.

Claune: The 19th-century French phonetic spelling for *clown*.

Clown: An English word that first appeared in the 16th century, when it was more often spelled cloyne, cloine, or clowne. Its etymology has been traced back to the words *colonus* and *clod*, meaning "rustic, boorish, of the farm."

Clown Alley: Clowns' dressing room.

Cook House: Dining area for circus performers and personnel.

Come In: In American circuses, the time (about 30 minutes) between the gates being opened and the beginning of the show. The clowns do the warm-up.

Compline: Last of the traditional hours of the Daily Prayer, prayed at the end of the day before going to sleep.

Corporal: A square of linen on which sacramental vessels are placed, usually has a cross embroidered on the front edge.

Crucifer: One who carries the processional cross at a church service.

Cruet: A small pitcher made of glass to hold the wine for Holy Communion or the water for the cleansing of the chalice.

Deacon: Principal assisting minister at the Holy Communion.

Divine Office: The Daily Prayer of the Church. *Office* means "service."

Dog and Pony Show: A small circus.

Donikers: Restrooms.

Dressage: The art of showing trained horses.

Easter Vigil: Worship service on Holy Saturday evening between Good Friday and Easter. Often the early church baptized household members at this service.

Entrée: A circus clown act, some ten to twenty minutes in length, usually performed by a whiteface and an auguste clown and containing a fair amount of dialog.

Epiphany: From the Greek "to shine forth." Season of the church year connecting Christmas and Lent.

Equestrians: Performers who work with horses.

Eucharist: From the Greek "thanksgiving." The service of Holy Communion.

Ewer: A pitcher in which the water for baptism is brought to the font.

Fair Linen: A cloth of fine linen that covers the top of the altar on top of the frontal, hanging down at either end a short distance from the floor. It is usually embroidered with five crosses (at each corner and in the center) to represent the five wounds of Christ.

Finale: When all circus performers and animals take their last bow.

Finish Trick: The last trick of a circus act.

First of May: A novice, greenhorn, or first season of a show.

Fixer: Legal adjuster.

Flagon: A pitcher usually of silver to hold the wine before it is poured into the chalice for Holy Communion.

Flats: Flatcars on the show train.

Fliers: Aerialists, especially those in flying return acts.

Flying Squadron: First section of the show to reach the lot.

Fool: A person who seems to lack common sense and has poor judgment. In the middle ages the word was much less pejorative.

Frontal: A parament, usually in the color of the season of the church year, that covers the entire front of the altar.

Front Door: The main entrance.

Get With It: To work harder.

Gloria In Excelsis: Song of the angels, sung during worship.
"Glory to God in the Highest."

Grand Entry Parade: The beginning of each show when all circus performers and animals enter and parade.

Grandstand: The reserved-seating section in the main tent.

Grease Joint or Grab Joint: Eating stand.

Grind Show: A show presenting a continuous performance.

Grotesque: Clowns having unusual and exaggerated features on their faces as well as their costumes.

Guys: Heavy ropes or cables that guy-off, or brace, the center poles.

Hanswurst: Literally means "Jack Sausage." A comic stock character in the German and Austrian theater in the 16th–18th centuries.

Hey Rube: Battle cry of the circus in early days.

Hippodrome: The track between the seats and the performing rings where colorful spectacles are performed.

Hobo Clown: See Tramp Clown.

Host: Bread or wafer used in Holy Communion.

Howdah: A chair that is carried on the back of an animal, usually an elephant.

Intinction: The practice of dipping the host or bread into the chalice of wine and administrating both elements at once in Holy Communion.

Iron-Jaw: An acrobatic stunt using an apparatus that fits into the performers' mouths and from which they are suspended.

Jackpots: Tall tales about the circus.

Jack Pudding: English term for clown used in the early 1600s, meaning buffoon.

Jester: A hired entertainer at a nobleman's house or royal court who often posed as a fool. He created jokes about the governing of the people.

Joey: A clown. Named after Joseph Grimaldi, famous clown of the 18th century.

Jump: Distance from one city to another.

Jungle Buggy: House trailer.

King Pole: First center pole of a tent to be raised.

Kinker: Any circus performer.

Kyrie: From the Greek *kyrie eleison*, "Lord have mercy, Christ have mercy, Lord have mercy."

Layout Man: The lot superintendent who locates the tents.

Lead Stock: Any of the haltered animals other than horses.

Lectionary: A course of readings used in worship services throughout the year.

Lent: A forty-day period between Epiphany and Easter; a time of repentance and preparation.

Liberty Acts: Horses trained to work free in the ring.

Little People: Midgets or dwarfs.

Liturgy: From the Greek, "work of the people." The whole body of texts and music used for the worship of God.

Lot: Land leased by the circus for the day of the performance.

Lot Lice: Town natives who arrive at the circus early and stay late.

Magnificat: Song of Mary from Luke 1:46-55.

March: Street parade.

Marquee: A canopied entrance.

Matins: Morning prayer worship service.

Maundy Thursday: From the Latin "a new command." The new commandment given by Jesus is to love one another. This is the theme for the Thursday of Holy Week.

Mensa: Top of the altar.

Midway: Area in front of the main entrance to the circus.

Mime: From the Greek *mimos* and Latin *mimus*. Original meaning was "to imitate" and referred to a kind of farcical drama popular in the Middle Ages. Today used as a shortened form of *pantomime*.

Missal: Altar book containing the services of the church for the use of those who minister at the altar. A missal stand holds the missal.

Mud Show: A circus show that travels over land (with horses and wagons or trucks and trailers), not on rails (trains).

Narr: Clown-simpleton figure in German drama, named after a well-known natural fool, Claus Narr (1570–1615).

Narthex: The vestibule or entryway of a church.

Nave: From the Latin "ship." The part of the church building where the people sit.

Nunc Dimittis: Simeon's song from Luke 2:29-32. "Lord, let your servant now depart in peace."

Office of the Keys: The word *office* means "service" or "ministry." A ministry of unlocking repentant sinners from the bondage of sin and pronouncing to unrepentant sinners that they are still locked in sin.

Office Lights: Candles used for the office of daily prayer.

Pad Room: That part of a dressing room used by riding acts.

Pall: (1) A stiffened piece of cloth used to cover the chalice during Holy Communion, to keep foreign objects from falling into it. (2) A large cloth, usually white but can match the seasonal colors, to cover the casket and symbolize the Resurrection.

Pantomime: From the Latin *pantomimus*, meaning "to mime all." It refers to an actor who silently enacted all the roles in a story narrated by a chorus and accompanied by music.

Paraments: A general name for the cloths in the liturgical colors used on the altar, pulpit, and lectern.

Paschal: Having to do with Easter. A paschal candle is used during Easter season.

Paten: A plate used to hold the bread for Holy Communion.

Pentecost: The outpouring of the Holy Spirit in Acts 2. Season of the church year stressing the growth of the Christian church through the power of the Holy Spirit.

Perch Act: A balancing act involving apparatus upon which one performs while being balanced by another.

Pericope: Portions of the Bible that are appointed to be read in the worship services of the church.

Pickle Herring: A clown character in 17th- and 18th-century Dutch and German theater. Wore a large Tyrolean hat and a costume with enormous ruffs and carried a sword.

Pie Car: Dining car on the circus train.

Pierrot: A comic servant clown (French) who powered his face white and wore a fancy, loose-fitting costume.

Pratfall: A comic fall, specifically a fall on one's prat (buttocks).

Producing Clown: In American circuses, the clown who designs and stars in routines, and who also builds all the props that they require.

Psalter: A collection of the psalms, sometimes in metrical poetry and sung.

Purificator: A linen napkin used to wipe the rim of the chalice during the administration of Holy Communion.

Rag: Tent.

Red Wagon: Main office of the circus.

Refrain: A recurring textual or melodic phrase, often sung after each verse or group of verses or a psalm or canticle.

Rigging: Apparatus used by high acts.

Rodeo Clown: Comic character and performer in the American rodeo who often wears makeup and a baggy costume and engages the announcer and the audience in comic repartee. He has the servant role of protecting the riders from the animals.

Roman Riding: A rider standing on the backs of two horses.

Rosin Back: Horse for bare-back riding.

Rubrics: Directions for conducting the worship services for ministers and congregation.

Sacrament: An ordinary action when connected to the Word of God. Distills the essence of the gospel. Baptism and Holy Communion. Anglicans and Roman Catholics have seven sacraments.

Sacramental Lights: Candles placed near the ends of the altar and lighted only for worship service with Holy Communion. Sometimes called the eucharistic candles.

Sacristy: A room for the vesting of the ministers and their preparation for the service. Also a room for those who prepare the altar for Communion.

Sanctus: "Holy, holy, holy Lord, God of power and might." From Isaiah 6:3.

Sidewall: Side of the tent.

Shekels: Money in any form.

Soft Lot: A wet or muddy lot.

Spot: Placing circus wagons on the lot.

Stand: Any town where the circus plays.

Stations of the Cross: A devotion often used in Lent involving a walk around the interior of the church with stops or stations to meditate on Jesus' journey to the cross.

Strawhouse: A sell-out. Straw was spread on the ground for general admission.

Stole: A scarf of fabric in the liturgical color worn over the shoulders by ordained ministers. It symbolizes the yoke of ministry.

Sufferages: Short petitions in a prayer, often a responsive prayer.

Sunbursts: Highly decorated wagon wheels.

Superfrontal: A band of fabric that extends across the front of an altar.

Surplice: A full, ankle-length white vestment worn over the cassock by ministers of the service, whether ordained or unordained. A shorter version of the garment is called a cotta.

Tail-up: Command to an elephant to follow in line.

Tenebrae: From the Latin "shadows." A Holy Week service, usually on Good Friday evening, during which candles are extinguished following the reading of specific Bible passages, describing the abandonment of Christ.

Thurible: The container in which incense is burned. See Censer.

Tops: Tents.

Tramp Clown: Sometimes called hobo or Charley. This character clown came from the United States in the time of the Great Depression (1930s). Usually dressed in torn clothing; has a red nose and unshaven (darkened) face. Although he knows how tough life may be, the tramp clown always goes through life with a sense of hope.

Troupers: Circus people.

Trunk-up: Command to an elephant to raise the trunk in salute.

Turnaway: A sell-out.

Veil: A cloth covering for the chalice and paten.

Vespers: From the Latin "evening." An evening service of prayer.

Vicar: One who serves in place of another. In Anglican use, one who serves in place of the rector of the parish. In Lutheran use, a vicar is often an intern, a seminarian who serves a parish by assisting a pastor.

Vigil: The eve of a feast when anciently the church would watch through the night in preparation for the dawning day.

Wardrobe: All costumes, even those of elephants and other animals.

Whiteface: An elegant, elite, clown with a full white makeup. The whiteface uses the basic colors of black, red, or soft blue on the face to highlight expressions. In Christian clowning known as the Joy Bringer.

Windjammer: A member of the band.

Zany: Comic role, especially that of a servant.

Bibliography

Arthur, Don. *Illusions In The Round*. Jackson, Miss: Express Printing, 1993.

Bain, Roly. *A Call To Christian Clowning*. London: Marshall Pickering, 1993.

Barrett, C. K. *The Gospel According to St. John*. London: S. P. C. K., 1967.

Bauer, Walter; Arndt, Wiliam F.; and Gingrich, F. Wilbur. *A Greek-English Lexicon of the New Testament and Other Early Christian Literature*. Chicago: University of Chicago Press, 1957.

Bergler, Edmund, M.D. *Laughter and the Sense of Humor*. New York: Intercontinental Medical Book Corporation, 1956.

Bergson, Henri. *Laughter*. New York: The MacMillan Company, 1928.

Bimler, Richard. *Angels Can Fly Because They Take Themselves Lightly*. St. Louis, Mo.: Concordia Publishing House, 1992.

Bishop, George. *The World of Clowns*. Los Angeles: Brooke House Publishers, 1976.

Bretscher, Paul G. *The World Upside Down or Right Side Up?* St. Louis, Mo.: Concordia Publishing House, 1964.

Brokering, Herbert. *I Opener*. St. Louis, Mo.: Concordia Publishing House, 1975.

Brokering, Herb; Hardel, Dick; and Sewall, Penne. *Tag, You're It!* Minneapolis: Youth & Family Institute of Augsburg College, 1998.

Brokering, Herbert. *The Wet Walk*. Published for the All Lutheran Youth Gathering, "For All the Saints," held in New Orleans, 1976.

Brown, Francis; Driver, S. R.; and Biggs, Charles A. *A Hebrew and English Lexicon Of the Old Testament*. Oxford: Clarendon Press, 1962.

Burgess, Hovey. *Circus Techniques*. New York: Drama Book Specialists, 1976.

Buttrick, G. A., ed. *The Interpreter's Dictionary of the Bible*. New York: Abingdon Press, 1962.

Cohen, Daniel. *Creativity: What Is It?* New York: M. Evans, 1977.

Cormier, Henri. *The Humor of Jesus*. New York: Alba House, 1977.

Cook-Craft, Rupert and Peter Coates. *Circus: A World History*. New York: MacMillan, 1979.

Corrigan, Robert, ed. *Comedy: Meaning and Form*. San Francisco: Chandler Publishing Co., 1965.

Cousins, Norman. *Anatomy of an Illness as Perceived by the Patient*. New York: Bantam, 1981.

Cousins, Norman. *The Celebration of Life*. New York: Bantam Books, 1991.

Cox, Harvey. *The Feast of Fools*. Cambridge, Mass.: Harvard University Press, 1969.

Cranfield, C. E. B. and C. F. D. Moule, eds. *The Cambridge Greek New Testament Commentary–St. Mark*. Cambridge: University Press, 1963.

Creed, John Martin. *The Gospel According to St. Luke*. New York: St. Martin's Press, 1965.

Culhane, John. *The American Circus*. New York: Henry Holt and Company, 1990.

Danker, Fredrick W. *Jesus and the New Age*. St. Louis, Mo.: Clayton Publishing House, 1974.

Danker, Frederick W. and F. Wilbur Gingich. *Shorter Lexicon of the Greek New Testament*. Chicago: University of Chicago Press, 1983.

Demaray, Donald E. *Laughter, Joy and Healing*. Grand Rapids, Mich.: Baker Book House, 1987.

dePaola, Tomie. *Jingle the Christmas Clown*. New York: Scholastic, Inc., 1992.

dePaola, Tomie. *The Clown Of God*. San Diego: Harcore Brace and Company, 1978.

Disher, Maurice W. *Clowns & Pantomimes*. Salem, New York: Ayer, 1968.

Doran, John. *History of Court Fools*. New York: Haskell, 1969.

Dorcy, Jean. *The Mime*. New York: Speller, 1961.

Duncan, Lois. *The Circus Comes Home: When the Greatest Show on Earth Rode the Rails*. New York: Doubleday, 1993.

Enevig, Anders. *Let's Start a Circus*. New York: Van Nostrand Reinhold Company, 1973.

Erasmus, Desiderius. *The Praise of Folly*. New York: Penguin, 1971.

Fife, Bruce; Blanco, Tony; Kissell, Steve; Johnson, Bruce; Dewey, Ralph; Diamond, Hal; Wiley, Jack; and Lee, Gene. *Creative Clowning*. Colorado Springs, Colo.: Java Publishing Co., 1988.

Fox, Charles Philip. *A Ticket to the Circus*. Seattle: Superior Publishing Co., 1959.

Fox, Charles Philip and Tom Parkson. *The Circus in America*. Waukesha, Wis.: Country Beautiful, 1969.

Franzmann, Martin H. *Follow Me: Discipleship According to Saint Matthew*. St. Louis, Mo.: Concordia Publishing House, 1961.

C. Welton Gaddy. *God's Clowns*. San Francisco: Harper & Row, 1990.

Gaona, Tito with Harry L. Graham. *Born to Fly*. Los Angeles: Wild Rose, 1984.

Goodman, Joel, ed. *Laughing Matters*. Saratoga Springs, N. Y.: The Humor Project, 1984.

Hadas, Moses. *The Complete Plays of Aristophanes*. New York: Bantam Books, 1962.

Hanson, R. P. C. *The Acts*. The New Clarendon Bible Series. Oxford: Clarendon Press, 1967.

Hardel, Dick. "Looking at Life from under the Big Top," *Resources for Youth Ministry, Vol. 3*. St. Louis, Mo.: Board for Youth Services, Lutheran Church–Missouri Synod, 1982.

Hardel, Dick. "Saints Celebrate Now," *Resources for Youth Ministry*. St. Louis: Board for Youth Services, 1977.

Hardel, Dick. *Welcome to the Sawdust Circle Part I: A Theology of Clown Ministry*. Orlando, Fl., 1988.

Hardel, Dick. *Welcome to the Sawdust Circle Part II: Learning the Art of Clown Ministry*. Orlando, Fl., 1988.

Hick, John, ed. *The Myth of God Incarnate*. Philadelphia: Westminster Press, 1977.

Hubbard, Freeman. *Great Days of the Circus*. New York: American Heritage Publishing Co., Inc., 1962.

Hugill, Beryl. *Bring on the Clowns*. Seacaucus, N.J.: Chartwell Books, Inc., 1980.

Hyers, Conrad. *The Comic Vision and the Christian Faith: A Celebration of Life and Laughter*. New York: The Pilgrim Press, 1981.

Kehl, Tim. "Getting Started in Clown Ministry," *Shoddy Pad*. Nashville: United Methodist Communications, 1978.

Kelly, Emmett with F. Beverly Kelly. *Clown*. New York: Prentice Hall, 1954.

Kennedy, D. James. *Evangelism Explosion*. Wheaton, Ill.: Tyndale House Publishing, 1977.

Kipnis, Claude. *The Mime Book*. New York: Harper & Row, 1969.

Kittel, Gerhard, ed. *A Theological Dictionary of the New Testament. Vol. 1-9*, translated by Geoffrey W. Bromiley. Grand Rapids, Mich.: Wm. B. Eerdmans Publishing Co., 1968.

Kung, Hans. *The Church*. New York: Sheed and Ward, 1967.

Kunhardt, Philip B., Jr.; Kunhardt, Philip B., III; and Kunhardt, Peter W. *P. T. Barnum: America's Greatest Showman*. New York: Alfred A Knopf, 1995.

Kysar, Robert. *Augsburg Commentary on the New Testament– John*. Minneapolis: Augsburg Publishing House, 1986.

Kysar, Robert. "Christology and Controversy," *Currents in Theology and Mission*. St. Louis, Mo.: Faculty of Seminex, Vol. 5, Number 6, December 1978.

Kysar, Robert. *John, the Maverick Gospel*. Atlanta: John Knox Press, 1976.

Lester, Michael. *How to Have Fun with Your Body*. Boston: Houghton Mifflin Co., 1986.

Liebig, Ernie and Jean. *Clowning Is—*. Bullard, Texas: Happy Enterprises, 1980.

Lindemann, Fred H. *The Sermon and the Propers*. Vol. 1-4. St. Louis, Mo.: Concordia Publishing House, 1966.

Litherland, Janet. *The Clown Ministry Handbook*. Downers Grove, Ill: Meriweather Publishing, Ltd., 1982.

Lohse, Eduard. *History of the Suffering and Death of Jesus Christ*. Philadelphia: Fortress Press, 1967.

Loxton, Howard. *The Golden Age of the Circus*. New York: Smithmark, 1997.

Luoma, John. "The Emergence of the Clown," *The Cresset*. Valparaiso, Ind: University Faculty, November/December, #17, 1977.

Lutheran Book of Worship. Minneapolis: Augsburg Publishing House, 1978.

Lutheran Book of Worship Minister's Desk Edition. Minneapolis: Augsburg Publishing House, 1978.

Manson, T. W. *The Servant Messiah.* Cambridge, England: University Press, 1966.

McLelland, Joseph C. *The Clown and the Crocodile.* Richmond, Va.: John Knox Press, 1970.

McVicar, Wes. *Clown Act Omnibus.* Downers Grove, Ill.: Meriwether Publishing, Ltd., 1978.

Moltmann, Jurgen. *The Church in the Power of the Spirit.* San Francisco: Harper & Row, 1977.

Moody, Raymond. *Laugh after Laugh: The Healing Power of Humor.* Staunton, Va.: Headwaters Press, 1978.

Mordenski, Jan. *Gabella: The One True Clown.* Canfield, Ohio: Alba House Communications, 1979.

Moule, C. F. D. *The Origin of Christology.* Cambridge, England: University Press, 1977.

Moulton, W. F.; Geden, A. S.; and Moulton, H. K., eds. *A Concordance to The Greek Testament.* Edinburgh: T & T Clark, 1963.

Newton, Douglas. *Clowns.* London: Harrap & Co., 1958.

Nicoll, Allardyce. *Masks, Mimes, and Miracles.* 1931 reprint. New York: Cooper Square, 1968.

Nineham, D. E. *St. Mark.* Baltimore, Md.: Penguin Books, 1963.

Nouwen, Henri J. M. *Clowning in Rome.* Garden City, N. Y.: Image Books, 1979.

Perrone, Stephen P. and James P. Spata. *Send in his Clowns.* Colorado Springs: Colo.: Meriwether Publishing, Ltd., 1985.

Pfatteicher, Philip H. and Carlos R. Messerli. *Manual on the Liturgy, Lutheran Book of Worship.* Minneapolis: Augsburg Publishing House, 1979.

Polakovs, Nikolai. *Behind My Greasepaint.* London: Hutchison, 1950.

Prenter, Regin. *Creation and Redemption*. Philadelphia: Fortress Press, 1967.

Reed, Luther D. *The Lutheran Liturgy*. Philadelphia: Fortress Press, 1947.

Richardson, Alan. *A Theological Word Book of the Bible*. New York: MacMillan Co, 1963.

Samra, Cal. *The Joyful Christ: The Healing Power of Humor*. San Francisco: Harper & Row Publishers, 1985.

Sanders, Toby. *How to Be a Compleat Clown*. New York: Stein and Day, 1978.

Saward, John. *Perfect Fools*. New York: Oxford, 1980.

Shaffer, Floyd. *Clown Ministry Skits for All Seasons*. Loveland, Colo.: Group Books, 1990.

Shaffer, Floyd. *If I Were a Clown*. Minneapolis: Augsburg Publishing House, 1984.

Shaffer, Floyd. "The Clown, Another Fool for Christ's Sake," *Resources for Youth Ministry*. St. Louis, Mo.: Board for Youth Services, Lutheran Church–Missouri Synod, 1975.

Shaffer, Floyd and Penne Sewall. *Clown Ministry*. Loveland, Colo.: Group Books, 1984.

Speaight, George. The Book of Clowns. New York: MacMillan Publishing Co., Inc., 1980.

Stolzenberg, Mark. *Clown for Circus & Stage*. New York: Sterling Publishing Co., Inc., 1981.

Stolzenberg, Mark. *Exploring Mime*. New York: Sterling Publishing Co., Inc., 1979.

Sutton, Felix. *The Book of Clowns*. New York: Grosset & Dunlap, 1975.

Swain, Barbara. *Fools and Folly During the Middle Ages and Renaissance*. New York: Columbia University Press, 1932.

Swortzell, Lowell. *Here Comes the Clowns*. New York: The Viking Press, 1978.

Tappert, Theodore G., ed., The Book of Concord. St. Louis, Mo.: Concordia Publishing House, 1959.

The Holy Bible. New Revised Standard Version. Iowa Falls, Iowa: World Bible Publishers, Inc., 1989.

The Oxford English Dictionary, Vol. II, C. Oxford: University Press, 1978.

Toomey, Susie Kelly. *Mime Ministry.* Colorado Springs, Colo.: Meriwether Publishing, Ltd., 1986.

Towsen, John H. *Clowns.* New York: Hawthron Books, Inc., 1976.

Trueblood, Elton. *The Human of Christ.* New York: Harper & Row, 1964.

Uehling, Carl T. *Blood, Sweat & Love.* Philadelphia: Fortress Press, 1970.

Weiss, Helen S. *The American Way of Laughing.* New York: Bantam, 1977.

West, Morris. *The Clowns of God.* New York: Bantam Books, 1982.

Willeford, William. *The Fool and His Scepter: A Study in Clowns and Jesters and their Audiences.* Evansville, Ind.: Northwestern University Press, 1969.

Young, Robert. *Analytical Concordance to the Bible.* New York: Funk & Wagnalls Company, 1955.

other Resources

Web Sites

Cirque Du Soleil: www.cirquedusoleil.com

Clowns of America, International: www.coai.org
(Dedicated to the art of clowning and bringing joy to everyone. Clown history, Find a Clown, The New Calliope *magazine, Artist in Residence.)*

Clown supplies:
    www.bubbasikes.com
    www.clownsupplies.com
    www.clownsoport.com
    www.clowncostumes.com
    www.frecklesupplies.com
    www.jestintime.com
    www.sillyfarm.com
    www.mooseburger.com
    www.stuff4clowns.com
    www.spearshoes.com
    www.feathersthefancyclown.com
    www.tmyers.com
    www.CornerstoneProductions.net
    www.clownsandthings.com
    www.orientaltrading.com
    www.lynchs.com

Clown ministry: www.geocities.com

Graphics: www.circusweb.com

Tents: www.anchorinc.com

Educational entertainment: www.bigcatencounter.com

Circus Hall of Fame in Peru, Indiana:
www.miamicountylife.com/Peru_Circus

International Clown Hall of Fame in Milwaukee, Wisconsin:
www.clownmuseum.org (history, inductees, clown types)

International Clown Hall of Fame Bookstore:
www.webdom.com/chof/bookstore/bkcirc.html

International Shrine Clown Association: www.shrineclowns.com

Ringling Bros. and Barnum & Bailey Circus®:
www.ringling.com (news releases, show dates, history and
tradition, Clown Alley)

The Humor Project, Inc.: www.humorproject.com (Founded by
Dr. Joel Goodman. This is the only organization in the
United States dedicated to the positive use of humor.
Conferences, catalogs, bookstore, speakers bureau, and
much more.)

The Fellowship of Merry Christians: www.joyfulnoiseletter.com
*(Founded by Cal Samra. They have a wonderful newsletter
and a catalog full of humor resources.)*

Youth & Family Institute of Augsburg College:
www.youthfamilyinstitute.com *(Connects home and congregation as partners nurturing faith. The provide wonderful
resources for nurturing faith for families and small groups.)*

World Clown Association: www.worldclownassociation.com
(Provides instruction, history, and conferences.)

Videos and Films

Note to the Reader: I don't know whether all these videos or old films are still available. Some of the old films have been transferred onto videotape now. Because circus videos and clown videos do not have a large market, most video stores do not carry them in stock. But I have found that the local video rental store is very helpful in locating special videos and making them available for sale.

A Clown Is Born. Produced by Faith and Fantasy, Inc. Filmed by W. O. Mitchell. Distributed my Mass Media Ministries, 2116 North Charles Street, Baltimore, MD 21218.

A Fable. Available from Concordia Publishing House, 3538 South Jefferson Ave., St. Louis, MO 63118. Phone: 314-268-1000.

A Time To See. (Features Artist and Creative Thinker Reinhold Marxhausen.) Produced by Bankers Life–Nebraska. Order from Concordia University, Seward, NE. 1-800-535-5494.

Barnum's Big Top. The anthology series, *The American Experience,* Distributed by PBS Video. 1991, ISBN 0-7936-0634-9, For information call 1-800-424-7963.

Be a Clown. Kenneth Feld Presents Ringling Bros. and Barnum & Bailey Home Video, exclusively distributed by MCA Distributing Corporation, 1987. ISBN: 1-55658-055-X. Phone: 1-800-PLAY-FHE.

Cirque Du Soleil Presents Quidam. Columbia Tristar Home Video, 1999. ISBN: 0-7678-4012-7.

Cirque Du Soleil: We Reinvent the Circus. Distributed by PolyGram Video, New York, NY, 1992.

Clown. (Henry Fonda as Emmett Kelly from 1955 TV.) Available from Jim Ridenour, P.O. Box 10343, Sarasota, FL 34278.

Do You See What I See? (Presentation by Artist and Creative Thinker, Reinhold Marxhausen.) Available from Lutheran Visuals, 10466 Plano Road, Dallas, TX 75238.

Fools for Christ. Cathedral Films. Religious Film Corporation, Box 4029, Westlake Village, CA 91359.

Leave 'Em Laughing. (Story of Jack Thum, featuring Mickey Rooney, shown in the United States on CBS, 1981.) Home Video, Charles Fries Productions, Inc.

Let's Go to The Circus! Walt Disney Mickey's Fun Songs Series. (Features the great clowning of David Larible.) Distributed by Buena Vista Home Video, Burbank, CA 91521. ISBN: 1-55890-582-0.

Parable. Rolf Forsberg, producer. Distributed by Ecu-film, 810 12th Ave. S., Nashville, TN 37203.

Patch Adams. (Features Academy Award® winner Robin Williams.) Universal Studios, 1999. Internet address: www.universalstudio.com/home. ISBN: 0-7832-3744-8

That's Life. Produced by Faith and Fantasy, Inc., Distributed by Mass Media Ministries, 2116 North Charles Street, Baltimore, MD 21218.

The Art of Silence. (Features Marcel Marceau in 13 pantomimes.) Available from Encyclopedia Britannica Films, 1822 Pickwick Ave.. Glenview, IL 60025.

The Box. Produced by Farm Family Films. Distributed by Mass Media Ministries, 2116 North Charles Street, Baltimore, MD 21218.

The Circus Year in Review, Season 1988. Available from Jim Ridenour, P. O. Box 10343, Sarasota, FL 34278.

The Greatest Clown Acts of All Times. Kenneth Feld Presents Ringling Bros. and Barnum & Bailey Home Video. Family Home Entertainment, 1988. ISBN: 1-55658-265-X.

The Mark of the Clown. Produced by Faith and Fantasy, Inc. Distributed by Mass Media Ministries, 2116 North Charles St., Baltimore, MD 21218.

The Mime of Marcel Marceau: An Introduction to the Performing Art Series. Available from Instructional Media Center, University of Nebraska–Lincoln, 421 Nebraska Hall, Lincoln, NE 68583-0900.

The Most Death-Defying Circus Acts of All Times. Kenneth Feld Presents Ringling Bros. and Barnum & Bailey Home Video. Exclusively distributed by MCA Distributing Corporation, 1987. ISBN: 1-55658-056-8.

Audio Tapes

Note to the Reader: I do not know whether these tapes are still available. But they are very helpful and are worth searching for.

Goodman, Joel. *The Magic of Humor: A Ho-Ho-Holistic View*. Published in 1983 and distributed by the Institute for the Advancement of Human Behavior (IAHB), 4370 Alpine Rd., Portola Valley, CA 94025. Also check with the folks at The Humor Project (www.humorproject.com).

Montagu, Ashley. *Growing Young: The Functions of Laughter and Play*. Portola Valley, Ca.: IAHB, 1983.

Moody, Raymond. *Humor as Therapeutic Intervention*. Portola Valley, Ca.: IAHB, 1983.

Piaget, Gerald. *Paradox, Humor and Healing*. Portola Valley, Ca.: IAHB, 1983.

Shaffer, Floyd. *Clown Ministry—Continued Insights*. Four-tape series produced by Faith and Fantasy, Inc. Distributed by Contemporary Drama Services, Downers Grove, Ill., 1982.

Shaffer, Floyd, *The Complete Floyd Shaffer Clown Ministry Workshop Kit*. Six-tape series produced in 1979 by Dennis Benson, P. O. Box 12811, Pittsburgh, PA 15241.

Other Helpful Resources by Dick Hardel or from The Youth & Family Institute of Augsburg College

The following resources can be ordered directly from The Youth & Family Institute, either online (www.youthfamilyinstitute.com) or by calling the toll-free number (877-239-2492).

Blest Be the Pie That Binds
Dick Hardel

This book complies family faith stories and observations about parenting into short devotional stories, each with four or five family activities. It is for godparents, uncles, aunts, grandparents, as well as parents.

FaithTalk
Merton P. Strommen and Charles Bruning

This is a set of 192 faith sharing cards to provide opportunities for in-depth conversations between young people and adults. It includes 48 share cards in each of four areas: Memories, Etchings, Values, and Action. The handy blue canvas carrying case makes it easy to use during travel time, vacation time, small group Bible studies, and many more.

FaithTalk with Children
Dick Hardel and Deb Stehlin

In the same design as *FaithTalk*, this resource is for parents and other adults who live and/or work with children ages 3–10. It is a set of 96 Share Cards, 24 in each of four categories: Memories, Feelings and Actions, Wonder, and Growing Together. A colorful spinner shows children which kind of card to choose. It comes in a red canvas carrying case.

It's for L.I.F.E!
Dick Hardel and Jennifer Mull

Wellness is not the lack of illness, but a Christ-centered balance in seven areas of healthy life: emotional, social, spiritual, occupational, intellectual, environmental, and physical. Clown ministry and laughter is about helping people live well in Christ. This manual provides a basic foundation for a congregation to begin a wellness ministry serving the community.

Tag, You're It!
Herb Brokering, Dick Hardel, and Penne Sewall

The three amigos worked together to bring this fun book of modern parables, clown skits, and family faith activities for people to learn more about the basic theology of the Christian faith.

That It May Be Well with You!
Edited by Dick Hardel and Jennifer Mull

This short book is a collection of essays on the roles of a congregation in promoting wellness in families and communities. Clown ministries are about wellness.